BUILDING PROSPERITY

Building Prosperity

in a Canada Strong and Free

Mike Harris & Preston Manning

Ideas for a More Prosperous Nation

2006

Series editor: Fred McMahon
Director of Publication Production: Kristin McCahon
Coordination of French publication: Martin Masse

Design and typesetting: Lindsey Thomas Martin
Cover design by Brian Creswick @ GoggleBox
Editorial assistance provided by White Dog Creative Inc.

Date of issue: November 2006
Printed and bound in Canada

Library and Archives Canada Cataloguing in Publication Data

Harris, Mike, 1945-
        Building prosperity in a Canada strong and free /
Mike Harris & Preston Manning.

Co-published by Institut économique de Montréal.
Includes bibliographical references.
ISBN 0–88975–238–9

        1. Canada--Economic policy--21st century.   2. Canada--Politics and government--21st century.   I. Manning, Preston, 1942-   II. Fraser Institute (Vancouver, B.C.)   III. Institut économique de Montréal   IV. Title.

JL65.H35 2006   320.60971'09051   C2006-905301-4

CONTENTS

MIKE HARRIS

Mike Harris was born in Toronto in 1945 and raised in Callander and North Bay, Ontario. Prior to his election to the Ontario Legislature in 1981, Mike Harris was a schoolteacher, a School Board Trustee and Chair, and an entrepreneur in the Nipissing area.

On June 8, 1995, Mike Harris became the twenty-second Premier of Ontario following a landslide election victory. Four years later, the voters of Ontario re-elected Mike Harris and his team, making him the first Ontario Premier in more than 30 years to form a second consecutive majority government.

After leaving office, Mr. Harris joined the law firm of Goodmans LLP as a Senior Business Advisor and acts as a consultant to various Canadian companies. Mr. Harris serves as a Director on several corporate Boards including Magna International and Canaccord Capital Inc. and is Board Chair of the Chartwell Seniors Housing REIT. He also serves on a number of corporate Advisory Boards for companies such as Aecon and Marsh Canada. Mr. Harris also serves as a Director on the Boards of the Tim Horton Children's Foundation and the St. John's Rehabilitation Hospital.

He is also a Senior Fellow of The Fraser Institute, a leading Canadian economic, social research, and education organization.

PRESTON MANNING

Preston Manning served as a Member of the Canadian Parliament from 1993 to 2001. He founded two new political parties—the Reform Party of Canada and the Canadian Reform Conservative Alliance—both of which became the Official Opposition in the Canadian Parliament. Mr. Manning served as Leader of the Opposition from 1997 to 2000 and was also his party's critic for Science and Technology.

Since retirement from Parliament in 2002, Mr. Manning has released a book entitled *Think Big* (published by McClelland & Stewart) describing his use of the tools and institutions of democracy to change Canada's national agenda. He has also served as a Senior Fellow of the Canada West Foundation and as a Distinguished Visitor at the University of Calgary and the University of Toronto. He is currently a Senior Fellow of The Fraser Institute and President of the Manning Centre for Building Democracy.

Mr. Manning continues to write, speak, and teach on such subjects as the revitalization of democracy in the Western world, relations between Canada and the United States, strengthening relations between the scientific and political communities, the development of North American transportation infrastructure, the revitalization of Canadian federalism, the regulation of the genetic revolution, and the management of the interface between faith and politics.

ACKNOWLEDGMENTS

As usual, we have a number of people to thank. Former Fraser Institute Executive Director, Michael Walker, and the current Executive Director, Mark Mullins, were instrumental in initiating this project and guiding it. Fred McMahon of The Fraser Institute once again served as series editor. Martin Masse, Director of Research and Publication, the Montreal Economic Institute, generously lent us his considerable expertise and directed the translation.

For the chapter on internal trade, we owe a special debt of gratitude to Canada's pre-eminent expert on internal trade, Robert Knox, the senior federal official responsible for internal trade policy and the federal co-chair of the Federal/Provincial Committee of Officials on Interprovincial Trade (1986–92) and Executive Director of the Internal Trade Secretariat (1992–95), managing the negotiation of the Agreement on Internal Trade.

We also owe many thanks to Fraser Institute research analysts Jason Clemens, Amela Karabegović, Milagros Palacios, and Niels Veldhuis. We are grateful for Kristin McCahon's steering this project through the production process. Both Jean Marie Clemenger, Preston Manning's secretary and researcher, and Elaine Pritchard, Mike Harris's assistant, did exemplary work in keeping the project on track. White Dog Creative Inc. provided valuable editorial assistance. Suzanne Walters, Dean Pelkey, and Leah Costello of The Fraser Institute, and Phil von Finckenstein have contributed much to our work by managing communications and arranging CS&F-related events.

Of course, we take full responsibility for the ideas and interpretations presented here. While we have relied on the insights of many, we set the analysis and the policy choices this document reflects.

BUILDING PROSPERITY

EXECUTIVE SUMMARY

GOAL To ensure that Canadians have the highest level of economic freedom and prosperity in the world.

FOCUS Economic freedom—providing citizens with the opportunity and the means to make more of their own economic decisions—is an essential prerequisite to high levels of economic prosperity. Customs, institutions, laws, policies, and business and government practices that constrain economic freedom, also constrain economic growth and reduce the prospects for prosperity. In empirical studies in the world's top peer-reviewed academic journals, economic freedom has been shown to create investment, prosperity, competitiveness, and numerous other positive outcomes.

In this volume, we examine constraints on Canadians' economic freedom imposed by excessive levels of government spending and taxation, barriers to internal trade, and over-regulation of business. In all these areas, we find Canadians' economic freedom is unnecessarily limited and we recommend ways to reduce these limitations.

GOVERNMENT SPENDING AND TAXATION

Excessive government taxation and spending limit the economic freedom of individuals and businesses by reducing their incomes and transferring economic decision-making powers into the hands of politicians and bureaucrats. Based on our examination of some of the world's best research on the optimal size of government and structure of taxation, we offer the following conclusions and recommendations.

OPTIMIZING THE SIZE OF GOVERNMENT

1 The size of government may be defined in terms of the level of government spending as compared to the size of the economy, that is, the percentage of Gross Domestic Product (GDP) consumed by the public sector. There is an "optimal" size for government that maximizes economic growth and social outcomes. At present, governments in Canada consume about 39% of GDP. However, top peer-reviewed research on the optimal size of government indicates that the optimal size for economies like Canada's lies within the range of 20% to 35% of GDP. A government sector in Canada that consumed 33% of GDP would be within this range and much closer than 39% of GDP to the optimal level required to increase both prosperity and positive social outcomes. We therefore conclude that Canada should adopt this level as a target and hereafter propose measures to achieve that target level within six years.

2 In particular, we recommend that governments of all levels in Canada restrain spending increases to 0.9% per year over the next five years. This will reduce the size of government in Canada to one-third of GDP in fiscal year 2011/12 and shift about $388 billion in spending away from government and back into the hands of individuals, families, and wealth-creating, job-creating, businesses.

REDUCING TAXATION

There is a cost and a benefit associated with every form of taxation. Not all forms of taxation are equally efficient in raising revenues; not every tax reduction is equally effective in stimulating growth. Research into the efficiency of various taxes and tax-reduction measures leads us to believe that the "mix" of tax reductions recommended below would be most effective in stimulating Canada's economic growth.

BUSINESS TAX RELIEF

❖ Accelerate the elimination of all corporate capital taxes in Canada.

❖ Reduce corporate income-tax rates. Specifically, the federal government should reduce its rate to 12.0% from 21.0% over the next five years. The provinces are encouraged to reduce their corporate income-tax rates by a minimum of 30%, with a target rate of 8%.

❖ Eliminate the federal surtax on corporate income taxes.

❖ The federal and provincial governments should increase the amount of income eligible for the small-business tax rate (preferential) with a view toward ultimately eliminating preferential treatment.

❖ The five provinces that still apply their provincial sales tax to business inputs, British Columbia, Saskatchewan, Manitoba, Ontario, and Prince Edward Island, should take measures to exempt business inputs. Specifically, all provinces should harmonize their provincial sales taxes with the federal goods and services tax (GST), which already exempts business inputs.

PERSONAL INCOME TAXES

❖ The federal and provincial governments should move toward a single-rate personal income tax.

❖ For those jurisdictions that retain multiple rates of personal income tax, the thresholds of income at which the additional rates apply should be increased. (One of the problems currently seen in the Canadian personal income-tax system is that middle and upper personal income-tax rates are applied at relatively low levels of income.)

SAVINGS AND INVESTMENT TAXES

* Eliminate Capital Gains taxes. As a small, open economy that is experiencing difficulty in attracting business investment, it is critical that Canada as a whole implement and maintain a highly attractive investment climate.

* Retain competitive taxes for dividends and interest income. The ideal would be to move toward a single-rate, integrated, tax system.

* Eliminate contribution limits for RRSPs and RPPs. The majority of Canadians save exclusively in tax-deferred accounts such as RRSPs; thus, greater flexibility in their use would have beneficial effects.

* Introduce tax-exempt, pre-paid savings accounts. These vehicles are essentially the reverse of RRSPs in that the tax is pre-paid but the earnings are tax exempt, as are any withdrawals.

ELIMINATING INTERPROVINCIAL TRADE BARRIERS

Canada cannot achieve the goal of leading the world in prosperity and economic growth without greater freedom of trade and exchange *within our own country*. Despite our professed commitment to free trade, a significant number of interprovincial trade barriers remain in effect across Canada costing the Canadian economy billions per year. To ultimately remove these restrictions on economic growth and ensure free trade within Canada, we recommend the following.

1 ACCEPTANCE BY ALL PROVINCIAL AND TERRITORIAL
GOVERNMENTS AND THE FEDERAL GOVERNMENT
OF THE PRINCIPLE OF AN OPEN DOMESTIC MARKET
The governments would agree to:

* establish rules to define what would be considered a trade barrier;

* undertake to remove or change any measures, policies, or practices that create an unjustifiable barrier;

* support the creation of a quasi-judicial Canada Internal Trade Tribunal to enforce the trade rules;

* take the necessary legislative steps to ensure that rules can be enforced.

2 ESTABLISHMENT OF A CANADA INTERNAL TRADE TRIBUNAL
The purpose of the Tribunal would be to enforce the trade rules established under the principle of an open domestic market. It would be a standing tribunal that would hear, and act upon, complaints from individuals, businesses, or governments concerning government measures that may be barriers to trade, investment, and worker mobility.

3 ESTABLISHMENT OF A CANADA INTERNAL TRADE COUNCIL
The role of the Internal Trade Council, which should be made up of Ministerial representatives, would be to monitor the performance of Canada's internal markets, identify issues and impediments that need to be resolved, and sponsor initiatives, including the negotiation of multilateral and bilateral agreements, to resolve these issues. The Council would make annual public reports to governments and to the Council of the Federation.

4 CLARIFICATION OF THE FEDERAL POWER TO STRIKE DOWN INTERPROVINCIAL BARRIERS
Throughout the Canada Strong and Free series, we have vigorously argued that Ottawa should respect the division of powers in Canada's Constitution and stop interfering in areas of provincial jurisdiction. In internal trade, on the other hand, Ottawa has declined to clarify, use, or expand its own constitutional powers to remove inter-provincial trade barriers.

We recommend a federal reference to the Supreme Court, asking it to clarify the extent of the present federal commerce power (that is, the power of the federal government under the present Constitution to strike down interprovincial barriers to trade) and what kind of amendment would be required, if necessary, to give the federal government that power.

ELIMINATING EXCESSIVE REGULATION

Government regulations prevent individuals and businesses from freely making decisions or entering into agreements they otherwise would in the absence of regulation. Obviously some regulation of economic activity is necessary and beneficial but over-regulation imposes heavy costs on consumers and businesses and can severely limit economic growth.

After examining research into the regulatory burden borne by Canadian business in comparison to our international competitors, we recommend a fundamental change in the way Canada introduces, manages, and reforms regulations. These changes would ultimately revolutionize the regulatory structure of Canada, eliminate unnecessary regulations, reduce the number of bad regulations put on the books, and ensure a relatively short life for ill-advised regulatory intrusion.

RECOMMENDATIONS

❦ Follow up the Smart Regulation Initiative launched in 2005 by the federal government. The goal of the initiative, which involves all levels of government, is to improve the regulatory system in Canada by eliminating overlaps between different levels of government and its agencies and by updating old regulations to reflect the realities of today's fast-changing world. One of the principles of the Smart Regulation Initiative is to learn what the best practices in regulation are from both within Canada and around the world, and to make those best practices, common practices in Canada.

✤ Require government officials and interest groups proposing new regulations to submit detailed benefit/cost estimates, including estimates of compliance costs as well as administrative costs.

✤ Require Parliament and the legislatures, or their appropriate Scrutiny of Regulations Committees, to hold regular "delegislation/deregulation" sessions where the only item of business is to strike obsolete, unnecessary, and overly restrictive laws and regulations from the books.

✤ Incorporate "sunset" clauses into all regulations and regulatory regimes. While deregulatory exercises may periodically clear the regulatory underbrush, we recommend a structure to prevent future regulatory build-ups. All newly enacted or renewed regulations should automatically expire in five years unless renewed; this would allow government to regularly re-examine its regulatory structure and determine whether regulations still serve a useful purpose. All levels of government, as well as any government bodies charged with regulatory oversight, should put in place this requirement.

THE BENEFITS OF ECONOMIC FREEDOM

In the final section of this report, we cite international studies and comparisons that strongly demonstrate that the expansion of economic freedom reduces unemployment, poverty, and inequality, and facilitates economic growth, human development, and the expansion of other freedoms around the world.

But what are the benefits for Canadians? What might a tangible expansion of economic freedom in this country mean for you? Simply this: increased income and job opportunities as you participate in the best performing economy in the world; the benefits of financially sustainable social services; and a superlative quality of life for you, your family, your community, and your country.

Implementation of the recommendations of this report would increase your economic freedom and your family's economic freedom. That, in itself, is a valuable goal. You and your family, not bureaucrats and politicians, should be making your economic decisions. And as a result, you would see your prosperity grow. As extensive research on economic freedom shows, at the end of the day, individuals and families simply look after themselves better than governments can. The ingenuity and drive of individuals, families, and businesses, when economically free, foster innovation, create wealth, and increase prosperity.

Can and should more be done to expand economic freedom and other freedoms at home and broad, to support the exercise of freedom of scientific inquiry and the application of its results to economic progress, to increase the freedom and adaptability of labour markets as well as capital and trade markets, to ensure a broader distribution of the means of wealth creation to an increasing number of people, and to insure that economic growth is not purchased at the price of environmental degradation? Of course, and stay tuned!

But let us begin by doing something which we Canadians do very well—seriously searching for the right "balance." What balance between our public and private sectors will induce the best performance from Canada's economy? What division of effort and resources among our three levels of government will deliver the peace, order, and public services essential to our quality of life at the least cost and greatest responsiveness to our desires? What balance between "perfect" freedom and the constraints necessary in a complex society will generate the highest levels of wealth and job-creating economic performance?

In this report, we have provided our best answers to these questions along with recommendations for action based upon those answers. Depending on your values and perspective, your answers to these questions and recommendations for action may differ from ours. But let us all join in a serious national conversation about these questions in the months ahead, the objective being to achieve the best economic performance in the world in a Canada strong and free!

1 INTRODUCTION

AIMING FOR THE TOP

Our goal is a simple one: we wish to make Canada the very best place on the planet to live. Our intent throughout the Canada Strong and Free series has been to point toward the practical way to this objective.

This goal is not overly ambitious. As Canadians, we have already accomplished much. Yet the talents of our people and bounty of our land equip us to do more, to create nothing less than the world's best governed and most prosperous nation, enjoying the highest quality of life on earth. The recent election of a new federal government provides a particularly exciting and timely opportunity to overcome the absence of policy vision that for more than a decade has limited Canada's advance.

Volume 1 of the series, *A Canada Strong and Free*, drew the outlines of a fresh vision for the future. Subsequent volumes have translated that vision into practical, proven policy approaches. Volume 2 of the series identified ways we can enhance the experience of Canadian life by improving the delivery and financing of health care, education, child-care, and social assistance. Volume 3 proposed steps to ensure that Canadians live in the best-run, most democratic and responsive federation on the planet.

This, our fourth volume, now seeks for Canadians the best economic performance in the world. It is an essential complement to our second volume: a high quality of life cannot be accomplished or sustained without high economic performance. Likewise, it is a necessary companion to our third volume: just as responsive democracy requires robust political freedoms, world-leading economic performance requires world-leading freedom of economic choice and action. Political freedom and economic freedom are indivisible.

REBALANCING: THE KEY TO PROSPERITY

A distinguishing element in the Canadian character is our desire for "balance"—our wish to avoid extremes and find the right equilibrium between competing goals and alternative means in all our endeavours, whether personal or collective. Yet, as our previous volumes documented, Canadian public policy and its administration have developed numerous and crippling imbalances. If our vision for a better Canada is to be realized, these must be corrected.

The earlier volume entitled *Caring for Canadians in a Canada Strong and Free* tackled the question: "What is the most efficient balance of responsibility and resources among our three levels of government—federal, provincial, and local?" If this balance is less than optimal—if Canada's public sector at any level is less productive than it could be—then obviously Canadians are getting less "bang for their tax buck" than we ought to. That, in turn, impairs the efficiency of the Canadian economy as a whole.

For example, in providing health care, a social service central to quality of life, every other industrialized country with universal health coverage (and medical outcomes superior to ours) has a "two-track system." These achieve an efficient, effective balance between public and private providers in financing and delivering health care of the highest quality. In Canada, a monopolistic *Canada Health Act* prevents us from pursuing, let alone achieving, this balance. While restricting Canadians' freedom of choice in health care, it provides medical results measurably inferior to those in countries that take a more balanced approach.

A key objective in our aspirations for Canada, therefore, must be to clear away every obstacle to attaining the best possible balance between the public and private sectors in the delivery of effective, efficient social services.

What is true for Canadians' health, we argue in this volume, is equally true for Canadians' wealth. The key to a dramatic improvement in the national economy is to strike a new balance between our individual freedom to make our own economic decisions and the limits governments place on our choices. Balance must be restored in several important dimensions: between the public and private sectors' consumption and use of national wealth; in Canadians' right to trade with other Canadians; and between individual Canadians' freedom to make economic choices and governments' desire to make those decisions for them through regulation. In short, a new balance must restrain the hand of government in order to unleash what has been identified empirically as the single most significant contributor to enhanced prosperity: Canadians' economic freedom.

In Chapter 2, we examine this important concept more closely. We show how Canada ranks in economic freedom against our international peers and competitors. We marshal a large body of evidence to show how expanded economic freedom will significantly boost the prosperity and well-being of Canadians.

Freedom, of course, is relative. At one extreme, it may be indistinguishable from anarchy. At the other, an "overweight" government consumes too much national wealth, limiting both present and future prosperity. How much is "just right"? In Chapter 3, we examine the most advanced research on the optimal size of government. The results are unambiguous: Canada's public sector is too large in proportion to our wealth-producing private sector. We therefore propose a new target ratio between the size of our public and private sectors, one scaled to liberate Canadians' innate ability to enhance our prosperity.

To attain this prosperity-enhancing new balance, we propose in Chapter 4 a path that addresses not only the appropriate scale of public spending, but a major adjustment in the types of taxation that will raise the necessary funds for government with the least impairment of national prosperity. We examine the efficiency of various kinds of taxes and propose a measured program of reduction and reform designed to leave substantively more wealth in the hands of Canadians. We show how this can be done so as to increase, rather than decrease, the sustainability of essential social services that governments provide.

Having pointed to the optimal scale for government's role in attaining the greatest possible national prosperity—and identified ways to achieve that scale—the last two chapters of this volume address other critical limitations on Canadians' economic freedom.

In Chapter 5, we examine Canadians' freedom to trade with other Canadians. Here again, the current balance is out of whack. While the federal government has intruded into many areas of provincial jurisdiction over the years, it has also failed to act on an important responsibility of its own: protecting Canadians' rights to trade freely with each other wherever in our federation they may live. Provinces defend barriers to trade that protect powerful special interests at the expense of all Canadians—including their own citizens. This constitutes yet another imbalance in need of redress if Canadians are to achieve the prosperity to which we aspire.

Chapter 6 examines the evidence that where government pre-empts individual and corporate economic freedom, putting decisions in the hands of bureaucrats and politicians through excessive regulation, prosperity again suffers. Of course, just as the optimal size of government is not zero, neither is the optimal regulatory requirement zero. Once more, the right balance is needed. We show that in Canada the balance is off. We endorse measures to strike the right equilibrium between appropriate regulation and freedom of economic choice.

None of these efforts to rebalance the economic federation would be worth pursuing if their advantages were merely theoretical. We conclude by identifying both the economic and non-economic benefits that will flow from the expansion of Canadians' economic freedom as a result of implementing the recommendations in this report.

2 LIBERTY TO PROSPER

REBALANCING ECONOMIC FREEDOM

ECONOMIC FREEDOM

Economic freedom is the key to prosperity. In empirical studies in the world's top peer-reviewed academic journals, economic freedom has consistently been shown to create investment, increase prosperity, enhance competitiveness, and advance numerous other positive social outcomes. In contrast, customs, institutions, laws, policies, and practices in business and government that constrain economic freedom also constrain growth and reduce the prospect of prosperity.[1]

No nation that lacks economic freedom has ever consistently improved the material lives of its citizens. Nor, for that matter, has any such nation ever established a stable democracy that respected other freedoms. Freedom is not easily subdivided.

Canada owes much to a generally high degree of economic freedom—including our stable democracy and enviable prosperity. Canada is consistently in the top 10 of the world's economically freest nations, as measured by The Fraser Institute's annual report, *Economic Freedom of the World* (see sidebar, THE FRASER INSTITUTE'S ECONOMIC FREEDOM INDEX AND REPORT, pages 14–15). But "good" is a long way from "the best." Indeed, Canada ranks in the bottom half of the top 10 in the measure of the economic freedom we provide to people and enterprises. We can do better.

---

1 See, for example, Easton and Walker, 1997; Farr, Lord, and Wolfenbarger, 1998; Grubel, 1998; and Gartzke, 2005. For a summary of the literature, see Doucouliagos and Ulubasoglu, 2006.

Canada can and must strive to give its citizens the greatest degree of economic freedom in the world. That measure of freedom is an essential prerequisite to achieving both the world's highest levels of economic performance and its most democratic governance.

WHAT DOES ECONOMIC FREEDOM REQUIRE AND HOW IS IT CONSTRAINED?

Economic freedom means liberating citizens to make more of their own economic decisions. The idea necessarily implies a limited government: over-sized governments, those that over-tax or substitute their decision-making for individual initiative and choice, are a major constraint on economic freedom.

THE FRASER INSTITUTE'S ECONOMIC FREEDOM INDEX AND REPORT

Economic freedom unleashes the drive and ingenuity of individuals and has positive dynamic consequences throughout the economy. The Economic Freedom Index, pioneered and developed by The Fraser Institute and published in the annual report, *Economic Freedom of the World*, was designed to create an objective test for how free individuals, families, and business enterprises are to make their own economic decisions.

The Economic Freedom Index measures economic freedom using 38 data points in the following five key areas:

* Size of government (expenditures, taxes, and enterprise)
* Legal structure and security of property rights
* Access to sound money
* Freedom to trade internationally
* Regulation of credit, labour, and business.

The Index thereby provides both a description of an economy and, when individual variables are compared to those of competitors, a prescription for policy improvement. Nobel Laureate Douglass North has called the Economic Freedom Index the best available description of "efficient markets."

Economic freedom requires an incorruptible rule of law, one that protects both persons and rightfully acquired property and applies equally to the powerful and the weak. More exactly: "Individuals have economic freedom when property they acquire without the use of force, fraud, or theft is protected from physical invasions by others and they are free to use, exchange, or give their property as long as their actions do not violate the identical rights of others" (Gwartney, Lawson, and Block, 1996). Where rule of law is weak or corrupted, where property rights are weak or denied, economic freedom is not only constrained—it can scarcely exist.

Economic freedom requires sound money. Inflation is a form of silent expropriation, eroding the value of wages, savings, and property. When inflation is not only high but also volatile and unpredictable, individuals and enterprises cannot plan for the future; they are thus effectively denied the exercise of economic freedom. An unsound money

The genesis of the Index can be traced back to 1984. Michael Walker, then executive director of The Fraser Institute, in conjunction with Milton and Rose Friedman, started the Economic Freedom Project to enhance understanding of the concept of economic freedom, its linkages to political and civil liberties, and their role in influencing economic performance. Initial research involved 60 of the world's top thinkers, including several Nobel Laureates. In the intervening 22 years, top economists, political scientists, philosophers, and sociologists have refined both the understanding of economic freedom and our ability to identify when it exists in a place and when it does not. The Economic Freedom Project remains on the cutting edge of today's research into the factors of prosperity and has a broad, worldwide audience.

Following the project's research phase, *Economic Freedom of the World: 1975–1995* was published in 1996. Since then, the annually published index has been the subject of over 200 academic and policy articles. The International Monetary Fund (IMF) concluded in its most recent annual report, *World Economic Outlook: Building Institutions* (September, 2005), that the most important determinant of economic advancement is the quality of institutions in a country. As one of its measures of institutional development, the IMF selected the Index published by The Fraser Institute in *Economic Freedom of the World*.

supply or erratic and confiscatory monetary policy are therefore another major constraint on economic freedom.

Economic freedom is expressed in the freedom to trade, in its broadest sense: to buy, sell, exchange, and transport resources, goods, services, and information freely across domestic and international borders, and to make contracts concerning these transactions. Limits on trade, whether domestic or international, are a further serious constraint on the exercise of economic freedom.

Economic freedom requires that government regulation of credit, labour, and business be minimized rather than maximized. Governments not only limit domestic and international exchange, they may also develop onerous regulations that limit the right to gain credit, to hire or work for whom you wish, or to freely operate commercial enterprises. Excessive regulation of this kind once again constrains economic freedom.

Most importantly, economic freedom is not readily divisible. Nations that respect economic freedom in just one area, while constraining it in others, do not enjoy its great advantages. Conditions and policies that enhance economic freedom must be considered *in toto*, as an overall package. To attain the full prosperity of which we are capable, Canadians require the greatest possible degree of economic freedom across the board.

MEASURING THE ECONOMIC FREEDOM OF CANADIANS

Canadians are justly proud of our political freedoms. But what is our record when it comes to economic freedom? The Fraser Institute's annual report, *Economic Freedom of the World*, measures this equally important quality across 38 distinct variables in five different areas. Table 2.1 (pages 18–19) provides a summary of the latest outcomes of these measurements, revealing Canada's over-all rank compared to other OECD nations as well as the non-OECD economies of Hong Kong and Singapore. The result is unequivocal: on a scale where first place should be the goal, Canada's performance should be improved for the benefit of all Canadians.

1 SIZE OF GOVERNMENT

Overall, out of 32 economies considered, Canada comes in at tenth place in size of government. We have the eleventh highest marginal income-tax rate, and the share of our economy consumed by government is closer to the bottom of the stack than the top: in 22nd place out of 32 jurisdictions. In other words, Canada is far from the top of the class. In fact, we are relatively heavy taxers compared to other developed nations. This unnecessarily decreases Canadians' economic freedom, reducing our ability to make our own decisions with our own money and putting those decisions in the hands of politicians and bureaucrats.

This over-sized governmental sector, compared to our leading competitors and trading partners, constitutes a major constraint on our ability to achieve superior economic performance. If we are to attain the quality of life we aspire to, we must liberate more of our economy to create prosperity. This will require striking a better balance between the public and private sectors without damaging social services. The analysis and recommendations of Chapters 3 and 4 describe steps we can take to achieve this critical goal.

2 LEGAL STRUCTURE AND SECURITY OF PROPERTY RIGHTS

An impartial legal system and secure property rights are essential to economic freedom. But Canada's ranking in this crucial area shows alarming decline. As recently as 2000, Canada ranked fifth best internationally on legal institutions and secure property rights, tied with Austria, Switzerland, and the United Kingdom with a score of 9.3 out of 10. By 2004, our ranking had plummeted to fourteenth and our score to 8.4.

For lack of military interference in politics, and for law and order, Canada received perfect scores in both years; as did many other developed nations. However, Canada ranked sixteenth in protection of intellectual property, down from twelfth in 2004. Canada's score fell from 8.0 in 2000 to 7.5 in 2004.

TABLE 2.1: CANADA'S OVER-ALL RANK FOR ECONOMIC FREEDOM COMPARED TO

1 Size of Government			2 Legal System & Property Rights			3 Sound Money		
Score	Rank		Score	Rank		Score	Rank	
9.1	1	Hong Kong	9.2	1	Denmark	9.8	1	Sweden
8.2	2	Singapore	9.0	2	Netherlands	9.7	2	United States
8.1	3	Mexico	8.9	3	New Zealand	9.7	2	Ireland
7.6	4	United States	8.9	3	Iceland	9.7	2	Finland
7.4	5	Switzerland	8.9	3	United Kingdom	9.7	2	Greece
7.3	6	Turkey	8.8	6	Finland	9.7	2	Switzerland
6.7	7	Iceland	8.8	6	Germany	9.6	7	Denmark
6.7	7	New Zealand	8.8	6	Ireland	9.6	7	Spain
6.7	7	United Kingdom	8.8	6	Australia	9.6	7	Austria
6.6	**10**	**Canada**	8.7	10	Switzerland	9.6	7	Luxembourg
6.6	10	Japan	8.7	10	Austria	9.6	7	Belgium
6.5	12	South Korea	8.7	10	Norway	9.6	7	France
6.4	13	Ireland	8.7	10	Luxembourg	9.6	7	Singapore
6.1	14	Australia	**8.4**	**14**	**Canada**	**9.6**	**7**	**Canada**
6.0	15	Greece	8.1	15	Singapore	9.6	7	Italy
6.0	15	Portugal	8.1	15	Sweden	9.6	7	Japan
5.8	17	Poland	7.8	17	United States	9.6	7	Netherlands
5.8	17	Germany	7.7	18	France	9.6	7	New Zealand
5.6	19	Italy	7.6	19	Belgium	9.6	7	Germany
5.3	20	Hungary	7.6	19	Portugal	9.5	20	Portugal
5.2	21	Spain	7.5	21	Japan	9.5	20	South Korea
5.2	21	Austria	7.5	21	Hong Kong	9.5	20	Hungary
5.0	23	Luxembourg	6.6	23	Czech Rep.	9.4	23	United Kingdom
4.9	24	Finland	6.4	24	Hungary	9.3	24	Australia
4.9	24	Slovak Rep	6.4	24	Spain	9.2	25	Hong Kong
4.8	26	Netherlands	6.3	26	South Korea	9.2	25	Poland
4.7	27	France	5.8	27	Italy	9.0	27	Norway
4.6	28	Norway	5.8	27	Slovak Rep	9.0	27	Czech Rep.
4.4	29	Czech Rep.	5.8	27	Poland	9.0	27	Iceland
4.3	30	Belgium	5.6	30	Greece	8.8	30	Slovak Rep
4.2	31	Denmark	5.2	31	Turkey	7.9	31	Mexico
4.0	32	Sweden	4.5	32	Mexico	5.1	32	Turkey

Source: Gwartney and Lawson, 2006. Note that data is for 2004.

THAT OF OTHER OECD NATIONS, HONG KONG, AND SINGAPORE

4 Freedom to Trade Internationally			5 Regulation			Summary Index		
Score	Rank		Score	Rank		Score	Rank	
9.5	1	Hong Kong	8.5	1	Iceland	8.7	1	Hong Kong
9.3	2	Singapore	8.3	2	Hong Kong	8.5	2	Singapore
8.8	3	Luxembourg	8.0	3	United States	8.2	3	New Zealand
8.6	4	Ireland	7.9	4	New Zealand	8.2	3	Switzerland
8.5	5	Belgium	**7.8**	**5**	**Canada**	8.2	3	United States
8.4	6	Slovak Rep	7.7	6	Switzerland	8.1	6	Ireland
8.4	6	Netherlands	7.7	6	Australia	8.1	6	United Kingdom
8.3	8	Hungary	7.6	8	United Kingdom	**8.0**	**8**	**Canada**
8.3	8	Austria	7.6	8	Singapore	7.9	9	Iceland
8.3	8	Czech Rep.	7.3	10	Hungary	7.9	9	Luxembourg
8.2	11	Germany	7.3	10	Luxembourg	7.8	11	Australia
8.0	12	New Zealand	7.2	12	Denmark	7.7	12	Austria
8.0	12	Sweden	7.2	12	Finland	7.7	12	Finland
8.0	12	Spain	7.0	14	Ireland	7.7	12	Netherlands
7.9	15	Denmark	7.0	14	Netherlands	7.6	15	Denmark
7.9	15	Finland	7.0	14	Japan	7.6	15	Germany
7.9	15	United Kingdom	6.8	17	Slovak Rep	7.5	17	Japan
7.8	**18**	**Canada**	6.7	18	Norway	7.4	18	Hungary
7.8	18	France	6.7	18	Spain	7.4	18	Portugal
7.7	20	Switzerland	6.7	18	France	7.3	20	Belgium
7.7	20	Portugal	6.7	18	Austria	7.3	20	France
7.6	22	United States	6.7	18	Sweden	7.3	20	Sweden
7.5	23	Italy	6.5	23	Portugal	7.2	23	Norway
7.3	24	Australia	6.5	23	Belgium	7.2	23	Spain
7.2	25	Mexico	6.4	25	Czech Rep.	7.1	25	South Korea
7.2	25	South Korea	6.2	26	Italy	6.9	26	Czech Rep.
7.2	25	Greece	5.9	27	Poland	6.9	26	Italy
7.1	28	Norway	5.8	28	South Korea	6.9	26	Slovak Rep
7.0	29	Poland	5.8	28	Germany	6.8	29	Greece
7.0	29	Turkey	5.7	30	Greece	6.7	30	Poland
6.7	31	Japan	5.5	31	Mexico	6.6	31	Mexico
6.4	32	Iceland	5.3	32	Turkey	6.0	32	Turkey

In two other subindexes, our nation suffered serious declines in both score and ranking. In 2000, the independence of Canada's judiciary scored 9.2 out of ten, earning a rank of sixth, tied with New Zealand; four years later, our score had fallen to 7.6 and our ranking to fifteenth place. For impartial courts, we had a score of 9.2 in 2000, placing Canada in a four-way tie for fourth spot with Germany, Ireland, and New Zealand. By 2004, our score had declined to 6.9—tying us for eighteenth spot with France. Both these falls are extremely troubling.

This document focuses on economic policy. A full discussion of our legal system would require a separate study. Nonetheless, the integrity and overall effectiveness of our legal system are essential not only to our economic well-being but also to many other aspects of our lives. Canada's decline in this area should raise a national alarm. We call for a thorough investigation into why the reputation of Canada's legal system is slipping.

3   ACCESS TO SOUND MONEY

Canada has solved (at least for the time being) what was once a dangerous problem that threatened our economic security: the erosion of sound money through inflation. Canada is in a multi-way tie for seventh spot on sound money, with a score of 9.6 out of 10. This is our highest score in any area of the Index by more than a full point. Moreover, the 0.2 point by which we trail world leader, Sweden, is the closest we come to top spot in any area of economic freedom.

We approve of, and support, the overall monetary course Canada is following to preserve its sound currency and, thus, will make no recommendations in this area. It must be noted, however, that our good performance on sound money is hardly superlative: virtually all other developed nations have scores about as good as Canada's. In short, Canada's competence in this area, while important, confers no special advantage against the nations that are our main competitors.

4 FREEDOM TO TRADE INTERNATIONALLY

As a trading nation whose economic prosperity is strongly linked to international commerce, Canada's score in this area is especially disappointing. We have persistently ranked down near twentieth spot among OECD nations plus Hong Kong and Singapore. This is not impressive in a field of 32 jurisdictions.

This year, Canada is in a tie with France for eighteenth place in freedom to trade, with a score of 7.8 out of 10. That is a drop of 0.5 points—and six places—since 2000, when Canada was in a three-way tie with Denmark, Spain, and Sweden for twelfth spot, scoring 8.3.

Canada's opportunity to trade is immense. In an era of relatively inexpensive global transportation, we sit between the great markets of Europe and Asia. We share an open border with the world's largest economy, that of the United States. Canadians should lead the world in our freedom to trade internationally. Instead, our ranking over the last four years is dismal—and declining.

Canada's first problem in this area, despite our professed commitment to trade liberalization, is our high and variable tariff wall. Overall, Canada's tariff barriers rank us nineteenth internationally, tied with New Zealand. Our regulatory barriers to trade are also relatively high, placing us in a four-way tie for fifteenth spot with the United States, Slovak Republic, and Hungary.

A future volume of the Canada Strong and Free series will offer concrete ideas for improving Canada's international trade significantly as part of a program to give our nation a stronger leadership role on the world stage. In this volume, we will discuss a dimension of trade not directly measured by the Economic Freedom Index but significant nonetheless to a large federation like ours, with distinctive regional economies and numerous provincial boundaries. That is: restrictions on internal trade. Canada cannot achieve the world's best economic growth unless it first accomplishes greater freedom of exchange within our own country.

5 REGULATION OF CREDIT, LABOUR, AND BUSINESS

Excessive government regulation of economic activity represents yet another serious constraint on economic performance. Again Canada's rank, as measured by the Economic Freedom Index, is decidedly B-team. Among OECD nations plus Singapore and Hong Kong, Canada ranks fifteenth behind Sweden, Belgium, and Italy in the amount of time business people must spend with bureaucrats to navigate regulatory hurdles. This is time they cannot spend building their enterprise and creating jobs.

More shocking is Canada's poor score in "irregular payments" required to secure regulatory approvals—in other words, corruption. In this sub-index, Canada ties for eighteenth place, in the bottom half of nations compared. This is the worst performance among nations with an "Anglo-Saxon" economic heritage.

Given that the data on irregular payments is based on a survey, information on the details of this problem is lacking. A full inquiry into the international perception of the need for "irregular payments" in Canada is beyond the scope of this report. But once again, the evidence of our low standing raises a flag. We note that further investigation is required.

CONCLUSION

In this chapter, we have laid out the importance of economic freedom and measured its extent in Canada by international comparison. In the league of developed countries with whom we compete most directly, our performance is only middling.

We believe Canadians deserve to be as economically free as the top jurisdictions. In the following chapters, we examine our key deficiencies in more detail, and identify steps Canada can take to attain the economic freedom necessary to achieve a world-leading standard of prosperity.

3 "RIGHT-SIZING" GOVERNMENT

REBALANCING THE PUBLIC AND PRIVATE SECTORS

GOVERNMENT SPENDING: SIZE MATTERS

The size of government, defined as the level of government spending compared to the size of the economy, has an impact on Canada's ability to achieve high rates of economic growth and social progress.

Most Canadians correctly view government as a positive force in the economy. Very few would argue for zero government involvement. On the other hand, most Canadians would also agree that governments can become too big. Indeed, history has proven that a completely government-controlled economy is not conducive to economic and social well-being. Somewhere between the two extremes of zero government involvement and a completely government-controlled economy exists a point at which economic growth and prosperity are maximized; this is what economists refer to as the optimal size of government.

The notion of an optimal size of government raises several questions: How can we know what size of government is optimal or "just right" for a country, in terms of maximizing economic growth and social progress? How big is government in Canada—and is its spending at the optimal level? If not, how should we go about reaching the optimal level? We attempt to answer all of these questions below.

How much a government spends in any country is, of course, a political compromise. Most countries are made up of citizens with different preferences. Some voters will want to keep government spending to a minimum while others favour more government involvement. Regardless of differences over the degree of government involvement, however, we believe most Canadians agree in desiring the highest level of economic and social progress attainable.

To that end, we reiterate our observation in the first volume of this series, *A Canada Strong and Free*: Canada needs an open, honest, and vigorous debate about the optimal size of government (Harris and Manning, 2005). That debate, moreover, should be conducted on the basis of sound empirical research.

1 THE OPTIMAL SIZE OF GOVERNMENT

Economists often use an upside down "U" curve to explain the notion of the optimal size of government. In Figure 3.1, the vertical axis measures the rate of economic growth or any other socio-economic value we wish to maximize. The horizontal axis measures the level of government spending as a percentage of gross domestic product (GDP), the value of all the goods and services produced by an economy.

FIGURE 3.1: THE OPTIMAL SIZE OF GOVERNMENT

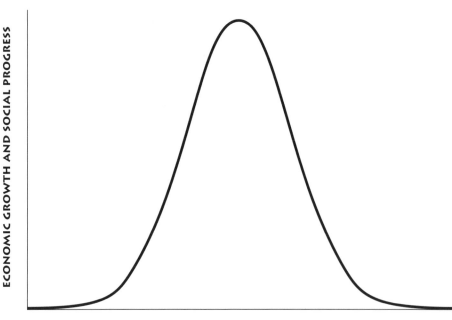

ECONOMIC GROWTH AND SOCIAL PROGRESS

GOVERNMENT SPENDING AS A PERCENT OF GDP

The shape of the curve can best be explained using a simple analogy (Walker, 1997). Think of government spending as a factor of production, like the use of fertilizer in agriculture. The initial use of fertilizer on a piece of land increases its agricultural output. As more fertilizer is added, agricultural output continues to increase but at a decreasing rate. At some point, the amount of fertilizer applied is optimal: any increase or decrease will lower agricultural output. Eventually, if enough fertilizer is applied, the excess will poison the field and nothing will grow.

Likewise, with zero government involvement in the economy, the level of basic public services is insufficient to sustain prosperity: economic growth and social progress are low. Initial government spending tends to finance services that promote economic freedoms: the maintenance of a legal system, protection of persons and property, a sound currency, essential transportation infrastructure, and basic education. These lead to greater economic growth and social progress. As the size of government continues to increase, rates of growth and progress also rise, albeit more slowly. At the top of the inverted "U" curve, government spending is optimal: beyond this point, more government spending will actually reduce the rate of economic growth and may impede rather than impel social progress. The tax revenues being collected to support that excess government spending would be more productive if the money were left in the hands of individuals and business to spend or invest as they see fit.[1]

2 SIZE OF GOVERNMENT AND ECONOMIC GROWTH

That is the theory. But where, exactly, is the top of the "U" curve? A growing body of empirical research into the impact of government spending on economic growth is illuminating the answer.

---

1 The composition of government spending is also important: for example, spending to ensure access and efficiency in the judiciary and the proper protection of people and property is highly effective. Spending on business subsidies and other grants to business may not be efficient.

Studies tend to focus primarily on the United States. For example, Richard Vedder and Lowell Gallaway (1998) investigated the size of the US government and its effect on economic growth for the Joint Economic Committee of the US Congress. Among their many findings was that moderate down-sizing of the federal government between 1991 and 1997 increased economic growth. They concluded that down-sizing government further still would also be growth-enhancing (Vedder and Gallaway, 1998). In the view of these researchers, cutting the size of the US government to 17.45% of GDP would produce sizable and permanent increases in GDP.

Gerald Scully of the University of Texas (Dallas) reviewed six decades of historical data to investigate what level of aggregate tax burden maximized the rate of economic growth in the United States. Using data for the years from 1929 to 1989, Scully concluded that the growth-maximizing tax rate was between 21.5% and 22.9% of gross national product (Scully, 1995).

Two studies have examined the size of government in Canada. Economists Herbert Grubel and Johnny C.P. Chao compared the size of government in Canada to economic growth rates between 1929 and 1996. They concluded that economic growth was maximized when governments consumed approximately 34% of GDP (Chao and Grubel, 1998). Using a different methodology, William Mackness examined spending and growth between 1926 and 1996; he concluded that economic growth was greatest when total government spending was in the area of 20% to 30% of GDP (Mackness, 1999).

In addition to these single-nation studies, a number of scholars have analyzed data for multiple countries. For example, Harvard economist Robert Barro investigated a wide range of variables in an attempt to determine their effect on economic growth in different jurisdictions. When investment in such services as education and defence was excluded from government spending, he found a "significantly negative association" between the share of a nation's economy represented by government consumption and GDP growth (Barro 1991: 430).

Gerald Scully explored the relationship between tax rates, tax revenues, and economic growth for 103 countries. He found, in general, that economic growth was maximized when governments took no more than 19.3% of GDP (Scully, 1991).

Stefan Folster and Magnus Henrekson (2001) examined the growth effects of taxation and government spending in "rich" countries and again found a strongly negative relationship. In fact, they found that for every 10% increase in government's consumption of GDP, economic growth fell by 0.7 to 0.8 percentage points (Folster and Henrekson, 2001).

Most recently, Afonso, Schuncknecht, and Tanzi (2005) analyzed the performance and efficiency of the public sectors in 23 industrialized countries. They found that "countries with small public sectors report the 'best' economic performance." When government spending exceeds 30% of GDP, economic growth declines. Strikingly, the researchers also concluded that "spending by big governments could be, on average, about 35% lower to attain the same [public sector performance]" (Afonso, Schuncknecht, and Tanzi, 2005: 337).

3 SIZE OF GOVERNMENT AND SOCIAL PROGRESS

The foregoing studies confirm that more government spending does not necessarily lead to greater economic growth. In fact, spending beyond the optimal level lowers economic growth. Many people argue, however, that societies trade off a small amount of economic growth in order to achieve greater social progress. But empirical studies do not confirm this relationship.

"Social progress" may, of course, mean different things to different people. But one important study by Gerald Scully attempted to aggregate many views by examining 16 different indicators from 112 countries including literacy, infant mortality, life expectancy, caloric consumption, access to health care, infrastructure, political freedom, civil liberties, and economic freedom. Using data for 1995, Scully compared countries whose governments spent less than 40% of GDP to those whose governments spent more than 50% of GDP; he found little or no difference in social outcomes (Scully, 2000). Indeed, for advanced countries on average, Scully could find no meaningful progress on these 16 social indicators for government spending that rose above 18.6% of GDP (Scully, 2000). There is some variance among countries. For instance, the rate at which government spending ceases to provide any marginal benefits in Canada is 19.5% of GDP.

Likewise, Vito Tanzi and Ludger Schuknecht studied social progress in 17 industrialized nations. They also found that governments spending more than 50% of GDP did not significantly outperform those spending less than 40%. In fact, not only did "large government" countries fail to progress faster than "small government" countries, but countries with "medium"-sized governments (spending between 40% and 50% of GDP) also did no better (Tanzi, 1995; Tanzi and Schuknecht, 1997a, 1997b, 1998a, 1998b).

4 THE "RIGHT SIZE" OF GOVERNMENT FOR CANADA

On the basis of these independent studies, we conclude that there is in fact such a thing as an "optimal" size for government, beyond which any increase or decrease in spending reduces economic growth. In addition, there is considerable evidence that this "optimal" point is at the smaller end of the scale of government size rather than the larger. That is, "small" governments that still provide critical public services achieve the same or greater social progress as "large" or even "medium"-sized governments.

The foregoing studies suggest that the optimal range for government spending is likely between 20% and 35% of GDP. While this "right size" will vary from country to country and even vary over time, the estimates suggest that the optimal scale for government in Canada is at the upper end of this range.

GOVERNMENT SPENDING IN CANADA
RELATIVE TO COMPETITOR COUNTRIES

The OECD estimates that Canada's governments spent 39.3% of our GDP in 2005. Figure 3.2 ranks this percentage with that of 27 other industrialized countries. The comparison reveals that Canada maintained the ninth smallest government, spending slightly below the OECD average of 40.7% of GDP.

However, Canada spends more on government than its chief trading partner, the United States, where governments consume only 36.6 % of GDP. Likewise, Canada's government sector is substantially larger than that of Australia (34.9%), an economy that shares many characteristics with Canada's. Other notable comparisons include Ireland (34.6%) and Japan (36.9%).

FIGURE 3.2: GOVERNMENT SPENDING AS A PERCENTAGE OF GDP, 2005

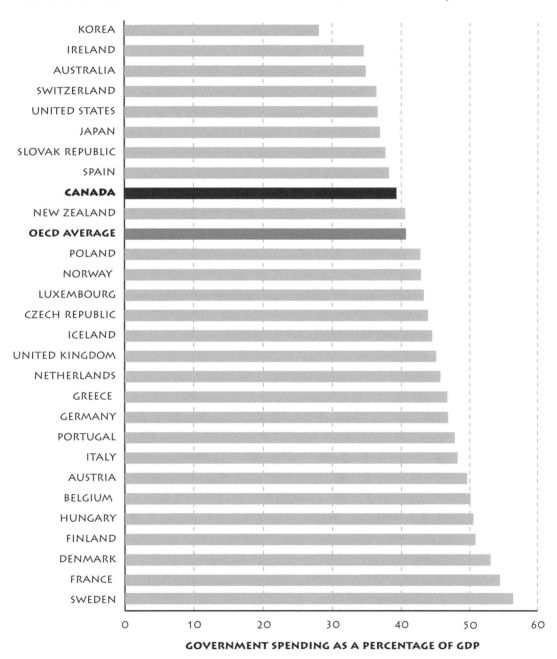

GOVERNMENT SPENDING AS A PERCENTAGE OF GDP

Source: Organisation for Economic Co-operation and Development, 2006.

Figure 3.3 presents an historical perspective on government spending relative to the economy in both Canada and the United States. It reveals that government in Canada has historically been much smaller than it is today. From 1930 to 1965, apart from the period of the Second World War, our government spending fell within 20% to 30% of GDP. Interestingly, Canadian and American governments during this period were roughly the same size, in percentage-of-GDP terms.

Beginning in 1965, however, Canada experienced a dramatic growth in government that continued for the next 27 years, opening up a significant gap relative to the United States. By 1992, that gap had reached 14.8 percentage points and Canada's government sector was consuming 38.5% more of our GDP than the US government did of America's. Since then, Canada has reduced the size of its government from 53.3% to 39.3% of GDP; the gap with the United States has narrowed but not closed.

FIGURE 3.3: GOVERNMENT SPENDING AS A PERCENTAGE OF GDP IN CANADA AND UNITED STATES, 1929–2005

Sources: Organisation for Economic Co-operation and Development, 2006; US Department of Commerce, Bureau of Economic Analysis, 2006.

The most important comparison however, is not the size of government in Canada relative to other countries, or even over time, but rather to empirical estimates of what an optimal scale of government might be for us. The studies referred to above put this scale in the range of 20% to 35% of GDP. Taking the upper end of this range as a fairly conservative optimal figure, government in Canada today is at least 13% larger than it need be to maximize economic growth and social progress.

BENEFITS OF REDUCING THE SIZE OF GOVERNMENT

The trend in the size of Canada's government from the 1960s onward is not unique. Indeed, from 1960 to the mid-1980s, government spending as a percent of GDP increased dramatically in most industrialized countries (Tanzi, 2005). In fact, most countries' governments continued to grow well into the 1990s, albeit more slowly. However, a recent study published by the International Monetary Fund (Schuknecht and Tanzi, 2005) found that the governments of most industrialized countries stopped growing sometime between 1982 and 2002. Many then began to shrink quite dramatically. This study, in particular, provides us with good evidence of what happens to economies and societies when governments retrench.

Schuknecht and Tanzi determined that most OECD nations had reduced the size of their governments between 1982 and 2002. For instance, government spending as a percentage of GDP in Ireland decreased by 16.4 percentage points from its 1982 peak to 2002. The GDP share of Canada's governments dropped from a high of 52.8% in 1992 to 41.4% ten years later—a decline of 11.4 percentage points. All told, six countries cut their government spending by more than 10% of GDP. Six more cut spending by 5% to 10% of GDP (Schuknecht and Tanzi, 2005).

Tanzi and Sckuknecht sorted these countries into two general groups: "ambitious" reformers and "timid" reformers. Countries were considered "ambitious" if the reduction in their government spending exceeded 5% of GDP. Reformers were also split into "early" actors (countries whose spending peaked by the early to mid-1980s) and "late" actors (those whose spending continued to rise into the early to mid-1990s).

Canada was classified as an "ambitious" but "late" reformer; our government spending reached a maximum of 52.8% of GDP in 1992, decreasing to 41.4% by 2002.

Sckuknecht and Tanzi then examined the impact of reduced government spending on a host of indicators. Contrary to the fears of many, these did not include declines in economic growth. To the contrary, in most cases economic growth actually improved after reforms. In addition, economic growth rose twice as fast among ambitious reformers as it did among timid ones. Employment displayed similar results, with ambitious reformers again enjoying greater improvement than timid nations. Examining socio-economic indicators, the authors found that the negative effect on income distribution from reduced government spending was small and, in fact, was largely mitigated by higher rates of economic growth and more targeted public spending.

Another important study, "Public Sector Efficiency: An International Comparison" (Afonso, Schuknecht, and Tanzi, 2005), measured the performance and efficiency of the public sectors in 23 industrialized countries in 1990 and 2000. The authors calculated indexes for two indicators: Public Sector Performance (PSP) and Public Sector Efficiency (PSE). For the first of these, the authors used seven sub-indicators, covering administrative, educational, health, and public infrastructure outcomes, as well as income distribution, an indicator of economic stability and another for economic performance. They found "notable but not extremely large differences in PSP across countries" (Afonso, Schuknecht, and Tanzi, 2005: 326). In general, "small" governments (spending less than 40% of GDP) performed better on the index than either "medium" (40% to 50% of GDP) or "large" governments (those consuming more than half their nations' GDP).

Canada's Public Service Performance rating for 2000 was the same as the United States'—a tie for twelfth place among the 23 countries studied. Both nations scored slightly above the group average.

The authors next used government spending as a percentage of GDP to calculate different countries' cost of achieving their measured Public Sector Performance. Using both total spending and spending for specific purposes (goods and services, education, health, public investment) as a basis, this produced their second index—Public Sector Efficiency. Here, the authors find more significant differences. Canada, for instance, ranked tenth among the 23 countries for its Public Sector Efficiency, just above the average but much lower than the United States (fifth). Once more, "small" governments scored higher in Public Sector Efficiency than "large" or "medium" ones did.

Finally, the authors measured "wastefulness" in public spending. In keeping with the other findings, small governments were much less wasteful than larger ones. Canada ranked twelfth in this calculation, with an input efficiency score of 0.75—meaning that Canada could attain the same public sector performance using only 75% of its current government spending.

CONCLUSION

Smaller public sectors, Tanzi and Sckuknecht have found, generally perform better than medium-sized or big governments. Their evidence indicates that Canada could attain the same public service performance it does today with significantly less government.

In 2005, Canada's federal, provincial, and local governments consumed 39.3% of our national income, according to OECD estimates. While this is the ninth-smallest government among 28 industrialized countries, it remains proportionately larger than those of the United States, Australia, Ireland, and Japan. More importantly, it is well beyond the level that maximizes economic growth and social progress.

Marked reductions in government spending as a share of GDP in many OECD countries have significantly improved fiscal, economic, human-development, and institutional performance indicators. We conclude that Canadians would benefit economically and socially from rebalancing the size of our government sector to an optimal level. In the next chapter, we recommend changes in public spending and taxation designed to increase Canadians' prosperity by optimizing the size of its government sector.

DATA USED TO ESTIMATE GOVERNMENT
SPENDING IN CHAPTERS 3 AND 4

To avoid confusion, it is important to note an important distinction between the source of data referenced in Chapters 3 and 4. In Chapter 3, we used data derived primarily from the OECD in order to provide international comparisons. Chapter 4 deals primarily with Canada alone. Hence, we use data drawn from Statistics Canada's Financial Management System to estimate spending from 2006/07 to 2011/12 more accurately .

This results in a slightly different estimate of the size of government than previously appeared. In 2005/06, the latest year for which Statistics Canada data is available, Canadian federal, provincial, and local governments spent a combined $546.9 billion. This amounted to 40.0% of GDP (compared to the figure of 39.3% that appeared in the Chapter 3).

As a basis for our analysis in Chapter 4, we also estimate a "status quo" level of growth in government spending from 2006/07 to 2011/12. We base this estimate on Statistics Canada's data for 2005/06 and assume that no major changes in spending are enacted. Specifically, we grow federal spending going forward by the average rate of growth from 2005/06 to 2007/08, as provided by the Federal Department of Finance (Canada, Department of Finance,2006). Growth in provincial and local government spending to 2011/12 is estimated using the average growth rate experienced over the past five years.

Our baseline calculations estimate consolidated federal, provincial, and local government spending at $575.0 billion in 2006/07, growing to $734.5 billion by 2011/12. Using this estimate, the size of government is expected to be 40.4% of GDP at the end of the five-year period (2011/12).

4 THE 33% SOLUTION

REBALANCING SPENDING AND TAXATION

HOW TO OPTIMIZE THE SIZE OF GOVERNMENT IN CANADA

It is evident that government in Canada consumes considerably more of our GDP than is needed to maximize economic growth and social progress. Estimates for Canada put the optimum somewhere between 20% and 35% of GDP. At present, our governments actually consume over 39% of GDP (see sidebar, DATA USED TO ESTIMATE GOVERNMENT SPENDING IN CHAPTERS 3 AND 4). In the first volume of the Canada Strong and Free series, we recommended that Canada move toward a government share of approximately 33% of GDP—one-third of the economy and roughly in line with the optimal size as estimated by Herbert Grubel and Johnny C.P. Chao (Chao and Grubel, 1998).

This will require adjustment. But change need not be wrenching. And it must be borne constantly in mind that the main objective of this adjustment is to attain for Canadians the highest standard of living and quality of life in the world.

We now wish to outline the shape and content of policies that would move us toward this goal. The changes we recommend apply to both sides of the fiscal ledger, to spending as well as taxation. Our target for achieving the necessary adjustment is the 2011/12 budget year—a five-year time horizon. We recommend that the restraint required to meet this objective be exercised at all levels of government.

We also note that the overall *rate* of taxation, as reflected in government's share of the national economy, is only part of the picture. The type of taxes employed to capture that share also matters. Therefore, we examine the current structure of government revenues in Canada and propose that reductions coincide with a rebalancing of taxation toward revenue sources that we believe would be most efficient.

CONSTRAINING PUBLIC SPENDING AND REDUCING TAXES

The goal outlined above is to rebalance the division of the Canadian economy so that more resources are left to private companies and individuals to spend or invest productively as they choose. This objective stands against a recent record in which government revenues at all levels have continued to increase, despite a number of important tax-rate reductions. Total government revenues in Canada have never been higher and are now over one-half trillion dollars. Happily, a relatively strong economy over the last decade has meant that these revenues represent a declining share of GDP. Much more is needed, however, to reduce the total size of government permanently and thus increase the share of the economy held in private hands.

Specifically, our objective requires a real reduction in the growth of government spending coupled with continued economic growth. Government spending need not be reduced in absolute terms but its growth needs to be slowed.

There are many ways governments might reduce their overall spending to 33% of GDP but all demand some measurable restraint in public spending. For instance, governments could aggressively reduce spending in the first year of our five-year horizon (2007/08) to immediately reach the 33% target. Alternatively, they might gradually achieve the same reduction over the full five-year period.

We recommend the latter strategy. Specifically, we propose that growth in consolidated federal, provincial, and local government spending be constrained to 0.9% per year for the next five years.[1] Under this

---

1   In the first volume of this series, *A Canada Strong and Free*, we estimated that government spending would have to be constrained to 1.6% increases. The reduced

scenario, government spending would grow from $575.0 billion in 2006/07 to $599.9 billion by 2011/12.

Table 4.1 presents the size of government from 2006/07 to 2011/12 under two different scenarios: growing spending using the "status quo" assumptions, and growing spending at 0.9% per year. An interesting calculation is the cumulative difference between the "status quo" level of government spending and the "constrained" level. This difference increases from $23.9 billion in 2007/08 to $134.7 billion in 2011/12. Over the five-year period, the cumulative difference amounts to $388.2 billion. In other words, reducing the size of government to 33% of GDP by 2011/12 would shift $388 billion in spending away from government and back into the hands of individuals, families, and wealth-creating, job-creating businesses.

EXAMINING THE STRUCTURE OF GOVERNMENT REVENUES

The adjustments we propose could shift more than one-third of a trillion dollars from the hands of bureaucrats and politicians to the private sector over five years. How that shift is accomplished is also significant. A reduction in the size of government on this scale provides an extraordinary opportunity not only to reduce taxation levels but also to reform the tax system.

In order to identify the most efficient mix of tax changes, we first examine how government revenues are presently structured across federal, provincial, and local levels—both in absolute terms and relative to national income. Next, we discuss the nature of taxation in Canada and review the literature on which types of taxes are least damaging to economic growth. We also compare the tax mix in Canada to that employed by our chief competitor nations. This analysis will set the context for the recommendations that follow.

---

level of increase reflected in the new estimate is due to recent and significant spending increases by the federal government and several provinces.

1 RATES VERSUS REVENUE: THE STILL-RISING COST OF GOVERNMENT

Tax cuts have been much discussed and widely promised in Canada over the last few years. Certainly, the previous federal government's professed commitment to a $100-billion tax cut, combined with major tax rate reductions in Ontario, Alberta, and British Columbia, have led to a popular impression that taxes have been reduced in Canada. In absolute terms,

TABLE 4.1: RESTRAINING THE SIZE OF GOVERNMENT IN CANADA

	2006/07	2007/08	2008/09	2009/10	2010/11	2011/12	Totals
(1) Size of government: "status quo" growth rates							
Total Spending (millions of dollars)	575,012	603,759	634,020	665,845	699,311	734,524	3,912,471
Percent of GDP	39.6%	39.8%	39.9%	40.1%	40.3%	40.4%	
(2) Size of government: constrained growth rates							
Total Spending (millions of dollars)		579,900	584,829	589,800	594,813	599,869	2,949,212
Percent of GDP		38.2%	36.8%	35.5%	34.2%	33.0%	
Difference in spending: (1) – (2)							
		23,859	49,191	76,045	104,497	134,654	388,246

Sources: Statistics Canada, Public Institutions Division, 2006; Canada, Department of Finance, 2006. Note: To calculate a baseline for overall federal, provincial, and local spending from 2006/07 to 2011/12 we use "status quo" growth rates. That is, federal spending is estimated using growth rates provided by the federal Department of Finance (2006 Budget) and provincial and local government spending is estimated using the average growth rate of spending from 2000/01 to 2005/06. In other words, the basis for our analysis assumes that federal spending grows in line with the federal government's own estimates and that provincial and local governments increase spending at the average rate experienced over the past five years.

this impression is wrong. While there have been important reductions in tax *rates* at both the federal and provincial levels, the amount of revenue collected has reached record highs.

Figure 4.1 illustrates the growth of total revenues at all levels of government in Canada combined, since the 1990/91 fiscal year.[2] Revenues are depicted in both nominal and inflation-adjusted (real) terms. Clearly, despite tax-relief measures enacted at various levels of government, revenues have continued their upward trend. Total government revenues increased at an average rate of 4.4% a year on a nominal basis, reaching $572.9 billion in 2005/06. When inflation is accounted for, the real growth rate is only somewhat less: still an average of 2.3% a year.

Figure 4.2 breaks down this overall growth in government revenue over the same period by level of government: federal, provincial, and local. Canada Pension Plan revenues, which consist primarily of compulsory contributions, are displayed separately. Plainly, very little has changed. In 1990/91, the federal government collected 42.0% of total tax revenues (47.2% including CPP/QPP revenues). Provincial governments collected 41.3%. Local governments collected only 11.5%. By 2005/06, the federal government collected a slightly smaller share directly, 39.9%, while still collecting 47.2% if CPP/QPP payments are included. Provincial governments collected slightly more, 42.7%, mostly at the expense of local governments, whose share dropped to 10.1%.

More significant than dollar increases, however, is the share of the economy (GDP) drawn off by governments. Figure 4.3 shows total government revenue as a percentage of nominal GDP between 1990 and 2007. Even though revenues increased in both nominal and inflation-adjusted terms over this period, consistent growth[3] meant that by the end, government consumed a smaller share of the economy. Specifically, total government

---

2 Revenue figures are consolidated and include the Canada Pension Plan (CPP) and Quebec Pension Plan (QPP).

3 Between 1990 and 2005, real GDP grew at an average annual rate of 2.6%. Since 2000, real GDP has experienced an annual growth rate of 3.0%.

FIGURE 4.1: TOTAL FEDERAL, PROVINCIAL, AND LOCAL REVENUES (NOMINAL AND ADJUSTED FOR INFLATION), 1990/91–2005/06

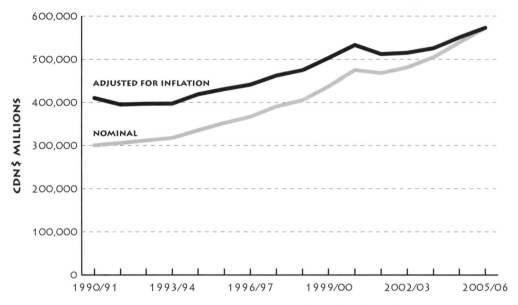

Sources: Statistics Canada, Public Institutions Division, 2003, 2004, 2005, 2006; The Fraser Institute.

FIGURE 4.2: NOMINAL REVENUES BY LEVEL OF GOVERNMENT, 1990/91–2005/06

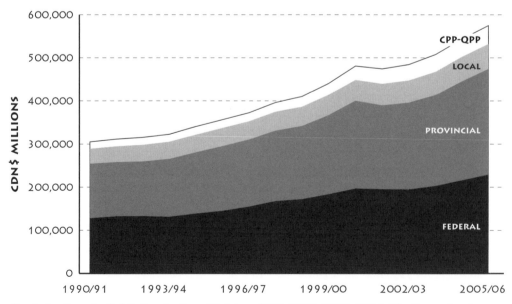

Sources: Statistics Canada, Public Institutions Division, 2003, 2004, 2005, 2006; The Fraser Institute.

FIGURE 4.3: TOTAL GOVERNMENT REVENUES (TAX AND NON-TAX RECEIPTS) AS A PERCENTAGE OF NOMINAL GDP, 1990–2007

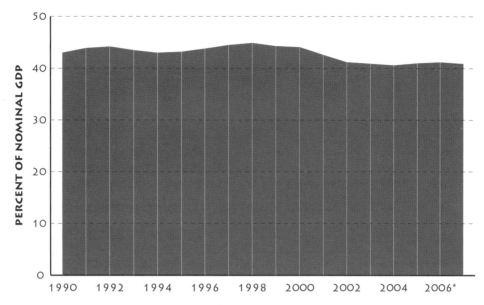

Source: Organisation for Economic Co-operation and Development, 2006.
Note: Values for 2006 and 2007 are forecasts.

revenues as a share of GDP peaked in 1998 at 44.9%. They have since declined to an estimated 41.0% of GDP in 2005, a decrease of 3.9 percentage points.[4] Once again, however, this decrease reflected strong economic growth rather than any actual decline in government revenues.

2 NOT EVERY DOLLAR ALIKE: HOW TAXES DIFFER

It is not only the overall burden of taxation that may constrain Canada's prosperity. Equally important is the structure of the tax burden, often called the "tax mix." Not all forms of taxation are equally efficient; similarly, not every tax reduction may be equally effective at stimulating growth.

---

4 Represents an 8.7% decrease in total government revenues as a share of GDP. It is important to note that Canada as a whole has moved from a marked position of deficit in 1990 of 5.8% of GDP to a surplus of 1.7% of GDP in 2005 (OECD, 2006).

Every tax imposes some economic cost, distorting the behaviour of individuals and businesses. Taxes on investment income (interest, dividends, and capital gains) for instance, decrease the after-tax rate of return; this leads to less saving and investment than would otherwise occur. Likewise, taxes on capital (corporate income and capital taxes) reduce the rate of capital accumulation so that, again, fewer resources are available for investment. Sales taxes distort consumption decisions. Taxes on labour incomes reduce take-home wages, discouraging effort and diminishing the number of hours worked. Research has consistently found that business or capital-based taxes impose significantly higher costs on an economy than do sales, payroll, or personal income taxes.[5]

These differences mean that reductions in various types of taxes also produce uneven effects. The federal Department of Finance, for instance, recently calculated the "welfare gain"—the increase in economic well-being—that would result from each dollar of reduction in various taxes (Baylor and Beausejour, 2004).[6] Differences were dramatic, as can be seen in Table 4.2. Each \$1 cut from personal income taxes on capital (dividends, capital gains, and interest income), offset by a \$1 increase in lump-sum tax revenues, led to a welfare gain of \$1.30. At the other end of the scale, \$1 cut from consumption taxes, similarly offset, produced the smallest benefit, a mere 10¢.[7]

Similarly, the economic cost of raising a dollar of revenue from one kind of tax may be different from that of raising a dollar from another.

---

5   For further information on the effects and costs of capital-based taxes, please see: Auerbach, 1983 and 1996; Beaulieu et al., 2004; Chirinko and Meyer, 1997; Chirinko et al., 1999; Cummins et al., 1996; Fazzari et al., 1988; Goolsbee, 1998, 2004a, 2004b; Razin and Yuen, 1996.

6   Benefits of different types of tax cuts were calculated by assuming that any revenue loss was offset by a non-distortionary "lump-sum" tax increase.

7   A number of other studies examine the economic or welfare costs of specific taxes in the United States: Feldstein, 1999; Gravelle, 2004, 1989; Gravellle and Kotlikoff, 1993; Cai and Gokhale, 1997; Lui and Rettenmaier, 2004; and Holtz-Eakin and Marples, 2001a, 2001b. For a summary of these studies, see US GAO, 2005.

TABLE 4.2: WELFARE GAINS FROM TAX REDUCTIONS[1]

Capital Cost Allowance	$1.40[2]
Sales Tax on Capital Goods	$1.30
Personal Capital Income Tax	$1.30
Capital Tax	$0.90
Corporate Income Tax	$0.40
Average Personal Income Tax	$0.30
Wage Tax	$0.20
Consumption Tax	$0.10

Source: Baylor and Beausejour, 2004.

Note 1: Revenue loss is assumed to be recovered through "lump-sum" taxation. Welfare gains are calculated as the gain in economic well-being per dollar of tax reduction.

Note 2: The estimate for an increase in capital cost allowances (CCA) is for new capital only. Increasing CCA is not a tax reduction per se but rather an increase in a deduction against corporate income taxes.

Most studies on the subject quantify this difference as the "marginal efficiency cost" (MEC) of a particular tax. Estimates of the MEC for Canadian taxes, based on another study from the Finance Department, are shown in Table 4.3.[8] Corporate income taxes are found to carry a much higher MEC ($1.55) than more efficient types, such as sales ($0.17) and payroll ($0.27) taxes. Both these studies concluded that consumption and payroll (wage) taxes impose lower economic costs than do capital-based taxes.

---

8   Among the most widely cited calculations of marginal efficiency costs are those completed by Harvard professor Dale Jorgensen and his colleague Kun-Young Yun (1991). Jorgensen and Yun's estimates of the MEC of select US taxes indicate a significant difference in the economic costs of different taxes. Specifically, corporate income taxes ($0.84) were shown to impose much higher costs than other more efficient types of taxes such as sales ($0.26). In other words, it costs the economy $0.26 to raise an additional dollar of revenue using consumption taxes and $0.84 to raise an additional dollar of tax revenue using corporate income taxes.

TABLE 4.3: ESTIMATES OF MARGINAL EFFICIENCY COSTS (MECS) FOR SELECT CANADIAN TAXES

	MEC ($CDN)
Corporate Income Tax	$1.55
Personal Income Tax	$0.56
Payroll Tax	$0.27
Sales Tax	$0.17

Source: OECD, 1997.

3 CANADA'S TAX MIX COMPARED TO THAT OF OUR CHIEF COMPETITORS

According to the most recent OECD dataset, the share of Canada's economy taken up by government ranks in the low mid-range of OECD countries: tenth out of 28 (Figure 4.4). At 41% of GDP, however, Canada's government revenue is higher than the average of 38% among OECD members, which include most of the world's industrial nations.[9] It is also higher than that of our biggest trading partner by far, the United States (32.8%).

In addition to collecting more than the OECD average in taxes overall, Canada is among the most reliant on the most economically damaging types of taxes. Table 4.4 breaks down how much revenue, as a percentage of the total, various industrialized countries collect from five different groups of taxes: income and profit, social security, payroll, property, goods and services, and other taxes. The comparison reveals that Canada is the fourth-highest user of the most damaging type of taxes, those on income and profit. Canadian governments collected 46.0% of their total revenue from those damaging tax types in 2003, fully one-third more than the OECD average of 34.4%.

At the same time, Canada makes relatively light use of more efficient revenue sources such as consumption taxes (referred to in Table 4.4 as "taxes on goods and services"). Governments in Canada collected only 26.1% of their revenues from efficient consumption taxes in 2003, compared to an OECD average of 32.1%.

---

9 Although Canadian governments spend 39.3% of GDP, government revenue equals 41% of GDP.

FIGURE 4.4: GENERAL GOVERNMENT REVENUES AS SHARE OF NOMINAL GDP, 2006

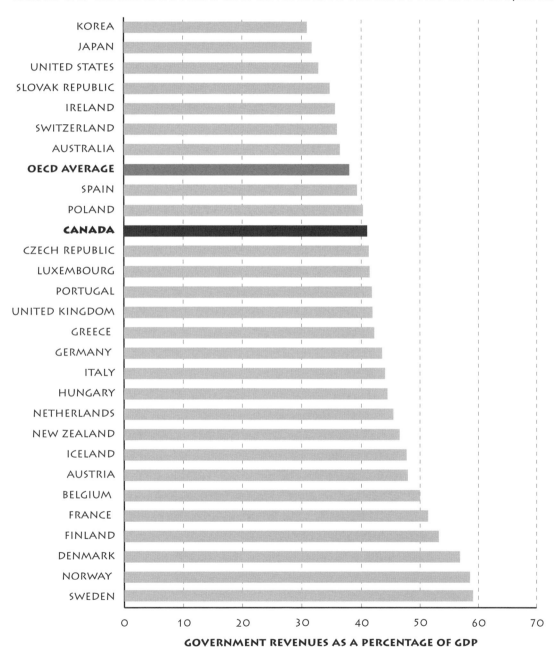

GOVERNMENT REVENUES AS A PERCENTAGE OF GDP

Source: Organisation for Economic Co-operation and Development, 2006.

TABLE 4.4: REVENUE, AS A PERCENTAGE OF THE TOTAL, COLLECTED FROM DIFFERENT TAXES (2003)

	Income and profit	Social security	Payroll	Property	Goods and services	Other
Poland	18.2	41.4	0.6	4.0	35.8	—
Slovak Republic	22.3	39.6	—	1.8	36.2	0.0
France	23.2	37.7	2.5	7.3	25.5	3.6
Greece	23.3	36.1	—	4.5	35.8	0.0
Turkey	23.7	20.8	—	3.2	49.5	2.9
Portugal	24.5	31.7	—	4.1	36.7	2.8
Hungary	24.8	30.5	2.5	2.2	39.4	0.7
Czech Republic	25.3	43.6	—	1.4	29.7	0.0
Netherlands	25.5	36.3	—	5.2	31.8	0.5
Mexico	26.5	16.9	1.8	1.6	52.5	0.7
Germany	27.4	40.5	—	2.4	29.4	0.0
Korea	28.0	19.5	0.2	11.8	37.1	3.3
Spain	28.2	35.3	—	7.5	28.2	0.5
Austria	29.7	33.7	6.2	1.3	28.2	0.7
Japan	30.6	38.5	—	10.3	20.3	0.3
Italy	30.9	29.5	—	8.0	25.7	6.0
OECD average	34.4	26.1	0.9	5.6	32.1	0.8
Luxembourg	36.3	27.9	—	7.5	28.1	0.1
Sweden	36.3	29.1	4.9	3.1	26.3	0.3
United Kingdom	36.5	18.5	—	11.8	32.7	—
Finland	38.7	26.7	—	2.3	32.0	0.1
Belgium	39.0	31.8	—	3.3	24.6	0.1
Ireland	39.3	14.8	0.6	6.5	38.4	—
Switzerland	42.9	25.5	—	8.3	23.3	—
United States	43.3	26.4	—	12.1	18.2	—
Norway	43.3	22.9	—	2.5	31.2	—
Iceland	44.3	8.6	—	5.9	41.0	0.2
Canada	**46.0**	**15.4**	**2.1**	**10.0**	**26.1**	**0.4**
Australia	55.2	—	5.6	9.5	29.7	—
New Zealand	59.6	—	—	5.2	35.2	—
Denmark	59.9	2.5	0.4	3.8	33.0	0.0

Source: Organisation for Economic Co-operation and Development, 2005.
Note: Categories may not add to 100.0 due to rounding.

RECOMMENDATIONS

The foregoing evidence is unequivocal. The difference in the economic impact of different types of taxes is striking: as much as $1.20 in economic welfare gained or foregone for each $1 tax cut, depending on which type of tax is reduced. At the same time, Canada stands dramatically apart from its OECD peers in relying disproportionately on the least efficient tax types.

Clearly, Canadians can choose to do better. As we observed at the outset of this chapter, Canada has an opportunity to improve its economic performance dramatically by changing its tax system in two ways. The first is to capture the increased prosperity that would flow from rebalancing our economy toward a more optimal size of government involvement through substantive reductions in the overall level of taxation. The second is to accomplish that reduction by cutting first and most those taxes that are most damaging to economic growth. Therefore, we make the following recommendations.

SIZE OF GOVERNMENT

We propose that growth in consolidated federal, provincial, and local government spending be constrained to 0.9% per year for the next five years. Under this scenario, government spending would grow from $575.0 billion in 2006/07 to $599.9 billion by 2011/12.

BUSINESS TAX RELIEF

There is no category of taxes in Canada in greater need of reduction than business taxes, broadly defined.[10] These levies, more than any other, prevent Canadians from achieving our full economic potential.[11] Remedies include the following.

---

10 For a thorough discussion of business taxes and the rationale for their reduction, please see Veldhuis and Clemens, 2006.

11 Jack Mintz, the eminent Canadian tax economist who headed up the influential federal Technical Committee on Business Taxation, has calculated that Canada has the second highest effective tax rate on capital investment among industrial countries (Mintz et al., 2005).

1 Accelerate the complete elimination of all corporate capital taxes.[12] This is largely a provincial issue, as the federal government has already committed itself to rapidly eliminate capital taxes.

2 Reduce corporate income tax rates. Specifically, the federal government should reduce its rate to 12.0% from 21.0% over the next five years.[13] The provinces are encouraged to reduce their corporate income-tax rates by a minimum of 30%, with a target rate of 8%. The cost of these reductions will vary dramatically by province since some (notably British Columbia, Alberta, and Saskatchewan) are already approaching the target rate.

3 Eliminate immediately the federal surtax on corporate income taxes.[14] This remnant of the deficit era of the 1980s and 1990s no longer serves a productive purpose. To the contrary, by increasing overall capital-based taxation, the surtax is extraordinarily costly and inefficient.

4 The federal and provincial governments should aggressively increase the amount of income eligible for the "preferential" small-business tax rate. Over time, this "preference" should be eliminated entirely, not by

---

12 A recent study (Veldhuis and Clemens, 2006) estimated that all governments in Canada would collect a total of $3.9 billion in corporate capital taxes in 2006/07. The total cost of eliminating corporate capital taxes over the five-year period was estimated at $12.0 billion.

13 The federal corporate income-tax reduction was estimated to cost $28.8 billion over five years (Veldhuis and Clemens, 2006). The provincial reductions were calculated to cost roughly $18.3 billion over the same five-year period (Veldhuis and Clemens, 2006). Veldhuis and Clemens (2006) provide a number of suggestions (such as closing preferential tax loopholes) to reduce the *net* cost of the suggested tax relief. The annual savings from these suggestions was estimated to be $6.2 billion in 2005/06 alone.

14 The 2006 federal Budget proposed eliminating the corporate surtax completely by 2008.

raising the small-business tax rate but rather by reducing the general corporate income-tax rate.[15]

5 The five provinces that still apply sales tax to business inputs, namely British Columbia, Saskatchewan, Manitoba, Ontario, and Prince Edward Island, should immediately end this practice. These provinces are further encouraged to harmonize their provincial sales taxes with the federal goods and services tax (GST), which already exempts business inputs. This would provide a double benefit by also reducing by one-half the paperwork required for businesses to collect and remit sales taxes. Provinces that implement exemptions without harmonization will not benefit from reduced administration and compliance costs, and could actually increase these costs.[16]

PERSONAL INCOME TAX RELIEF

After business, the revenue base next most in need of marked tax reduction is personal income. Personal income-tax rates in Canada are generally high and the incomes at which they are applied are relatively low. Substantial cuts in middle- and upper-bracket personal income-tax rates would harness the productive energies of workers, business owners, and entrepreneurs across the country. We suggest the following measures.

1 The federal and provincial governments should follow the lead of Alberta by moving toward a single-rate personal income tax. Removing the disincentives for work, saving, investment, and entrepreneurship inherent in increasing tax rates as incomes rise, will encourage productive activity and make the Canadian economy more efficient.

---

15 For further information on the small-business income-tax rate and the problems associated with large marginal increases as firms lose their eligibility for the lower rate, please see Hendricks et al., 1997 and Clemens and Veldhuis, 2005.

16 For an excellent discussion of this problem, please see Veldhuis, 2006.

2 For jurisdictions that retain multiple tax rates, it is critical that the thresholds at which higher rates apply be raised. One of the problems in the current Canadian personal income-tax system is that "middle" and "upper" income-tax rates are applied at relatively low levels of real income.

SAVINGS AND INVESTMENT TAX RELIEF

A number of changes could be made to the taxes levied on savings and investment that would yield sizeable benefits to the Canadian economy without sacrificing substantial amounts of government revenue. These include the following.

1 Eliminate capital gains taxes.[17] As a small, open economy struggling to compete for business capital, it is critical that Canada create and maintain a strongly attractive investment climate. Eliminating levies on capital gains would not only remove one of the most economically costly of tax types but also send a strong pro-development and investment signal to potential investors.

2 Retain taxes on investment income at competitive rates. The ideal would be to move toward a single-rate, integrated, tax system.[18] Failing that more fundamental reform, however, it is critical that Canada and its provinces ensure that our treatment of savings, dividend, and interest income remains strongly competitive internationally, especially with the United States.

3 Eliminate contribution limits for RRSPs and RPPs. The majority of Canadians save exclusively in tax-deferred accounts such as RRSPs. Greater flexibility in their use would have beneficial economic effects.

---

17 For further information on the benefits of eliminating capital gains taxes, please see Grubel, 2000, 2001, 2003.

18 For further information on integrated flat tax systems, please see Emes and Clemens, 2001 and Hall and Rabushka, 1995.

4 Introduce tax-pre-paid savings accounts. These are essentially the reverse of RRSPs, in that the tax is pre-paid but earnings are tax-exempt, as are any withdrawals.[19]

CONCLUSION

The size of Canada's government sector is clearly greater than the optimal point, identified in Chapter 3, that would maximize our nation's future economic performance and social progress. In this chapter, we have identified a practical target for rebalancing government closer to this optimal point of roughly one-third of the Canadian GDP.

The policies we have recommended are designed to reach this target in a practical and progressive way, restraining the growth of government spending to less than 0.9% per year over five years. This can and should be accomplished by reducing those taxes that most heavily penalize work, savings, investment, and entrepreneurship. The effect would be to transfer more than a third of a trillion dollars of economic decision-making power from the hands of bureaucrats and politicians to Canadian families, workers, consumers, and businesses.

What might this mean to the average Canadian? Simply this: increased income and job opportunities as you participate in the best performing economy in the world; the benefits of financially sustainable social services; and a higher quality of life for you and your family.

---

19 For further information, please see Kesselman and Poschmann, 2001.

5 FREE AT HOME

STRIKING DOWN BARRIERS TO TRADE IN CANADA

Liberty to work, trade, and do business with whom we prefer is a central component of economic freedom. It is essential to our goal of attaining for Canadians the greatest possible prosperity and quality of life.

In an upcoming volume of the Canada Strong and Free series dealing with ways that Canada can give stronger leadership on the world stage, we will offer concrete suggestions for improving our nation's position in international trade. Here, however, we draw attention to a type of restriction on trade that is not explicitly measured by the index published in *Economic Freedom of the World* but which nonetheless imposes very real costs upon a large federation like Canada, with our distinctive regional economies and numerous provincial boundaries. That is: restrictions on internal trade.

Canada cannot achieve the goal of leading the world in prosperity and economic growth without greater freedom of trade and exchange within our own country. In other words, Canada needs an open, efficient, and predictable domestic market in order also to improve its productivity and competitiveness in an increasingly globalized world. There would be ancillary benefits: more open trade at home would strongly reinforce the integrity of our federation as a true economic union.

The sadly balkanized state of Canada's domestic market, fragmented by persistent inter-provincial barriers to trade, is analyzed below. That discussion leads to recommendations for removing those barriers and achieving a freer domestic market.

BACKGROUND: A LEGACY OF RESTRICTION

Sir John A. Macdonald's "National Policy" created an economic environment that, in one form or another, dominated Canada for 80 years—until after the Second World War. This policy allowed Canadian business to develop behind high tariff walls. The immediate result was a high-cost manufacturing sector based almost exclusively in central Canada.

But the same policy had other negative consequences. It acted to discourage processing of natural resources in Canada, since products made by inefficient, tariff-protected manufacturers were seldom able to compete with foreign products. It protected certain farmers with "supply management" programs; these erected barriers to domestic trade and left a legacy of inefficient production that still demands protection. For Canadians, these policies have ultimately meant higher prices, lower wages, less consumer choice, and severely constrained productivity.

Canada was not alone in following this protectionist strategy. Other countries did the same, including the United States. But it was a strategy that allowed our governments to ignore the impact their policy choices were having on the efficiency of Canada's domestic market and our overall competitiveness (Hart, 2004: 8; Statistics Canada, 2002: Introduction, p.3).

Happily, federal governments in more recent years have stepped away from this nineteenth-century strategic thinking—albeit only partially. But among the provinces it remains disturbingly robust. This is despite the clear intent of Confederation's founders. Section 121 of Canada's Constitution in effect prohibits the erection of tariff-based barriers to trade within Canada. In a crucial oversight, however, it does not provide a mechanism to eliminate non-tariff barriers.[1] Moreover, this section does not cover trade in services or intellectual property.

The federal government has constitutional authority to regulate some key aspects of inter-provincial trade. It uses this authority in rela-

---

1 "All articles of the Growth, Produce, or Manufacture of any one of the Provinces shall, from and after the Union, be admitted free into each of the other Provinces" (*The Constitution Act*, 1867, Article 121).

tion to drugs, some aspects of trade in agricultural and food products, and the labeling of goods traded inter-provincially. But this federal authority cannot interfere with the right of provinces to regulate within their own areas of constitutional authority. Provincial governments, for example, have constitutional authority (sometimes shared with the federal government) to regulate workers, building standards, the environment, agricultural and food products sold within their borders, transportation, businesses, finance and securities, education, and alcoholic beverages.

For nearly 130 years, provincial governments have exercised these powers to maintain barriers to inter-provincial trade, investment, and labour mobility—all in the name of protecting local and provincial interests. The result is a mishmash of measures and standards that create resilient but virtually invisible non-tariff barriers in Canada's domestic market, with no effective incentive or mechanism to remove them. As one observer has said: "inter-provincial barriers to trade create an interlocking, tangled and expensive web of vested interests. Together they slowly and steadily choke Canada's economic arteries, losing output, incomes and jobs for Canadians" (Parsons, 1994: 2).

Three practices in particular create most of these internal barriers to trade: **1.** discriminatory rules, such as preferences based on provincial residency; **2.** differential standards or regulations that, for example, require different qualifications for identical occupations; and **3.** inequitable administrative practices, such as local worker requirements.

These barriers harm both consumers and producers. The additional costs are mostly borne by consumers while producers sell less due to higher prices. They reduce the ability of Canadian firms to trade in other provincial markets and limit their international competitiveness. The result is a less efficient economy than we could have. The costs to the Canadian economy are difficult to estimate. Whatever the real cost to Canadians, it is measured in billions of dollars per year.[2]

---

2 See Beaulieu, Gaisford, and Higginson, 2003, which provides a review of the literature on costs.

LOOKING ABROAD: CHANGING PATTERNS OF INTERNATIONAL AND DOMESTIC TRADE

Numerous studies and commissions over the years have identified barriers to interprovincial trade as a major impediment to the Canadian economy. The Rowell Sirois Commission identified them as an issue in 1940.[3] So did the Macdonald Commission in 1985.[4] In constitutional negotiations in 1980 and again in 1990, Canadian governments tried without success to agree on steps to free the domestic market.

By 1990 however, the pattern of Canada's overall trade began to change significantly. The tariffs that had protected Canada's domestic market for years, the residue of the old National Policy, were disappearing. This was particularly true for trade within North America, as a result of the Canada-US Trade Agreement (CUSTA) and the North American Free Trade Agreement (NAFTA). But it also followed from the introduction of the World Trade Organization (WTO). As the external tariff wall fell, internal barriers that reduce the productivity and the competitiveness of the domestic economy became correspondingly more important.

The change in trade that ensued was significant. In 1990, Canada's interprovincial and international exports were almost identical in volume. By 1995, interprovincial exports were only 62% of international exports, and had fallen still further to 44% by 2000. The balance swung somewhat back by 2005, when interprovincial exports amounted to 53% of international exports.

---

3   "The heart of the problem lies in the fact that the simplest requirements of provincial autonomy ... involve the use of powers which are capable of abuse ... The problem is to preclude or restrict abuses without interfering with legitimate and even necessary powers" (Canada, Royal Commission on Dominion-Provincial Relations, 1940).

4   "Federalism justifies variation among provinces in response to local preferences ... the need to accommodate diversity ... must be balanced against the objective of gains from trade" (Canada, Royal Commission on the Economic Union and Development Prospects for Canada [Macdonald Commission], 1985: vol. 3, pp. 135–40).

Viewed another way, international exports were 26.1% of GDP in 1989 and interprovincial exports, 22.1%. By 1997, international exports were 40.2% of GDP and interprovincial exports, 19.7%. By 2005, the levels were 37% and 20%, respectively.[5]

The increase in international exports has been driven by improved Canadian labour costs relative to the United States, reduced US tariffs, and the American appetite for imports (Grady and Macmillan, 1998: 26). The declining share of interprovincial exports in GDP is the result of lower Canadian tariffs (encouraging more international imports), slower growth in Canada than in the US market, and relatively small increases in the prices of goods traded interprovincially.

Interprovincial trade remains more regional than national in Canada. Trade is concentrated within four regions: the Atlantic provinces including Newfoundland and Labrador; central Canada, which is Québec and Ontario; the western provinces; and the North (Statistics Canada, 2002: 10). Domestically, the provinces and territories in these groupings trade mainly among themselves. Distance makes a difference; that is, the Atlantic region has the smallest trade with the western provinces and vice versa.

Despite the great distances of our geography and persistent internal non-tariff barriers, interprovincial trade remains a significant part of the Canadian economy. Studies in the 1990s determined that borders reduce trade between nations by more than would be expected on the basis of official barriers alone. This is because it is more expensive and difficult to trade internationally, where potential business partners may not be well-known to each other, than it is to trade at home, where partners are more likely to share common values, understandings, and circumstances (Helliwell and McCallum, 1995; Helliwell, 2002; McCallum, 1995). International trade contributes more to Canada's economy than ever. It could be more important still, if our domestic economy were more productive and efficient.

---

5   Comparative analysis of international and domestic trade data can be found in several studies from Statistics Canada including: Statistics Canada, 1998; 2000; 2002; 2004.

DASHED HOPES: EFFORTS TO FREE CANADA'S DOMESTIC MARKET

The Charlottetown Accord to amend the Constitution, which was accepted unanimously by Canadian governments on August 28, 1992, committed legislatures to remove barriers to the movement of persons, goods, services, and capital.[6] The Accord was defeated by a referendum on October 26, 1992.

Having failed to resolve the issue through constitutional change, Canadian governments turned to non-constitutional means (Knox, 1998). In December 1992, federal, provincial, and territorial trade ministers agreed to negotiate a comprehensive agreement to "promote an open, efficient and stable domestic market for long-term job creation, economic growth and stability." This was to be accomplished by reducing and eliminating "to the extent possible, barriers to the free movement of persons, goods, services and investments within Canada" ([Committee on Internal Trade], 1995): "Preamble," p. 1). First ministers signed the Agreement on Internal Trade (AIT) on July 18, 1994. It came into force on July 1, 1995.

The AIT includes general rules that establish reasonable principles for an open domestic market. Unfortunately, these apply only to specific sectors in a manner laced with qualifications, exclusions, and exceptions. Disputes under the agreement can only be directed to a complicated, time-consuming, and ultimately unenforceable resolution process. The AIT has changed some things. But governments have ignored many of its obliga-

---

6   "*Reducing Internal Trade Barriers.* Forging an economic union today means moving beyond a simple prohibition against interprovincial tariffs on goods towards free internal movement of persons, goods, services and capital. A new provision would reflect the commitment of governments to this objective. First Ministers have agreed to discuss how best to implement the principles of a stronger internal common market" (Canada, Intergovernmental Affairs, Privy Council Office, 2001).

tions, particularly those intended to extend its coverage. Ten years after it came into force, the agreement has proven to be ineffective. It is now being reviewed and revised by governments under the leadership of the Council of the Federation (CoF).[7]

Several provinces are also attempting to remove internal barriers to trade on bilateral terms through bilateral agreements. On April 28, 2006, for example, the Premiers of British Columbia and Alberta ratified a Trade, Investment and Labour Mobility Agreement, or TILMA (British Columbia, Ministry of Economic Development, 2006). This pact marks a significant improvement over the AIT. It is inclusive; that is, everything is covered unless specifically identified as an exception. It has one set of general rules and principles that apply to all government measures that relate to trade, investment, or labour mobility. It is comparatively simple and accessible. And, it has a single, shorter, and more accessible dispute-resolution process than the AIT, with consequences if a judgment is ignored.

While the Alberta/BC TILMA is an improvement on the AIT, it is not yet perfect. Both provinces identified numerous exclusions, even though many are temporary and all subject to regular review. Although its dispute-resolution process is simpler than that of the AIT, it will not necessarily be easier for a person or business harmed by a non-tariff barrier to use; the maximum penalty of $5 million for non-compliance is too low to deter the erection of every non-tariff barrier.

Barriers to internal trade, investment, and labour mobility continue to limit the productivity and competitiveness of Canada's domestic market. The initiatives just described and a number of recent studies (see sidebar, STUDIES IN SCLEROSIS: REPORTS ON INTERNAL TRADE IN CANADA, page 64, for a partial list) have served to clarify the problem. They also point the way to a number of conclusions and possible remedial measures.

---

7   The Council was established in December 2003 and is made up of the leaders of all of Canada's provincial and territorial governments.

CONCLUSIONS

Past and present efforts to liberalize internal trade in Canada, and the studies referred to above, suggest the following conclusions.

* Canada has an open and healthy domestic market that operates reasonably well, given our relatively small economy and large physical size.

* Although our domestic market is open and healthy, it is neither as open nor as flexible as it ought and needs to be. This is because of significant and complex non-tariff trade barriers between provinces that are a function of Canada's federal structure and the legacy of more than 100 years of protective trade policy.

* These barriers are not uniform but rather a mix of measures. Some are intended to protect local or special interests. Some result from differences among jurisdictions in standards and regulations. Still others arise from duplicative and protective administrative practices, at both the federal and provincial levels.

* Some barriers are obvious; others are almost invisible, embedded in long-standing and accepted interprovincial practice. Many of these seem intractable, protected by a culture of entitlement and a tradition of applying constitutional authority unilaterally rather than cooperatively. These attitudes may be rooted in historic regional differences and mistrust.

* These barriers, whatever their characteristics, continue to limit Canada's economic productivity and competitiveness. They reduce the ability of our businesses to adapt creatively and quickly to changes in world economic conditions, and to the needs of our main trading partners, particularly the United States.

* Canada lacks effective constitutional means to strike down barriers to trade in our domestic market. There is no constitutional obligation for Canadian governments to apply their authority in a way that does not cre-

ate such barriers or to avoid compromising the integrity and productivity of the national economy. Two attempts to strengthen the economic union and deal with non-tariff barriers, in 1980 and 1990, failed.

❧ Non-constitutional initiatives to eliminate domestic trade barriers, notably the 1995 Agreement on Internal Trade and ongoing efforts to establish some form of national regulation of financial securities, have met with very limited success.

❧ The Alberta/BC Trade, Investment and Labour Mobility Agreement (TILMA) is a step in the right direction. But, in the future negotiation of such agreements:

    ❧ no measure that can operate as a barrier to domestic trade should be excluded;

    ❧ any measure that constitutes such a barrier should be changed or removed unless it can be demonstrated that it is necessary to an essential public policy, and that it accomplishes this purpose in the least trade-restrictive way possible; and

    ❧ penalties for maintaining proscribed barriers, as assessed by any tribunal established under such agreements, should not be limited and should apply until the barrier is removed.

RECOMMENDATIONS

The abolition of costly and unproductive barriers to internal trade would significantly enhance the performance of the Canadian economy, both at home and in its international competitiveness. To that end, we recommend the following measures.

1 *Formal acceptance by all provincial and territorial governments and the federal government of the principle of an open domestic market*
The purpose of such acceptance would be to establish that all Canadian governments accept that measures they undertake must not operate as

barriers to trade, investment, and worker mobility. The governments would agree to:

* establish rules to define what would be considered a barrier; these might be similar to those in the current AIT;
* define under what circumstances a measure presenting a barrier to trade might be permitted; this could be based on the "legitimate objective" provision in the AIT;
* remove or change any measures, policies, or practices that create an unjustifiable barrier;
* support the creation of a quasi-judicial Canada Internal Trade Tribunal to enforce the foregoing trade rules;
* commit themselves to taking the necessary legislative steps to ensure that these rules can be enforced in relation to measures in their jurisdiction.

2 *The establishment of a Canada Internal Trade Tribunal*

The purpose of the Tribunal would be to enforce the trade rules established under the principle of an open domestic market. It would be a standing tribunal that would hear complaints from individuals, businesses, or governments against measures that may be barriers to trade, investment, and worker mobility.

It is assumed that governments will continue to enter into multilateral and bilateral agreements on matters such as public-sector procurement. The Tribunal could also provide an enforceable dispute-resolution mechanism for these agreements.

Ideally an existing body, such as the Canadian International Trade Tribunal, could serve as the Internal Trade Tribunal. A legal basis for the Tribunal we propose might be found under the federal power to legislate in relation to interprovincial trade. If not, it should be established by interprovincial agreement under the auspices of the Council of the Federation.

3 *The establishment of a Canada Internal Trade Council*

The purpose of the Internal Trade Council would be to provide an advisory and political forum for issues not covered by the general agreement referred to in Recommendation 1 above. As such, it should be made up of ministerial representatives from all governments.

Not all impediments to trade will be susceptible to challenge before the Internal Trade Tribunal. Issues such as public-sector procurement, business registration, and disclosure requirements affect the domestic market but will require a separate specific agreement to resolve. The same applies to many regulatory regimes that are better reconciled by agreement than through challenge before a panel.

The role of the Internal Trade Council would be to monitor the performance of Canada's internal market, identify issues and impediments that need to be resolved, sponsor initiatives including multilateral and bilateral agreements, and resolve these issues. The Council would issue annual public reports to governments and to the Council of the Federation.

4 *Investigation of federal constitutional powers in internal trade*
Throughout the Canada Strong and Free series, we have vigorously argued that Ottawa should respect the division of powers in Canada's Constitution and stop interfering in areas of provincial jurisdiction. In internal trade, on the other hand, Ottawa has declined to use its own constitutional powers, which are admittedly unclear, to remove interprovincial trade barriers.

Unfortunately, the use of this power involves a more difficult question than may first appear. Few trade barriers are erected specifically as "trade barriers," even if that is their intent. Instead, they are typically enacted under the guise of consumer protection or some other provincial power. Removing such barriers could thus be interpreted as an intrusion on provincial responsibility.

We recommend a federal reference to the Supreme Court asking it to clarify, first, the extent of the present federal commerce power (i.e., the power of the federal government under the present Constitution to strike down interprovincial barriers to trade) and, second, what kind of amendment would be required, if necessary, to give the federal government that power.

STUDIES IN SCLEROSIS
REPORTS ON INTERNAL TRADE IN CANADA

Beaulieu, Eugene, Jim Gaisford, and Jim Higginson (2003). *Interprovincial Trade Barriers In Canada: How Far Have We Come? Where Should We Go?* The Van Horne Institute.

COMPAS (2004). *Inter-Provincial Trade Barriers: Seriously Damaging to the Economy and Standard of Living and Almost as Harmful as Canada-U.S. Trade Barriers.* BDO Dunwoody/Chamber Weekly CEO/Business Leader Poll in the *Financial Post*, for Publication September 13, 2004. COMPAS Inc.

Canadian Chamber of Commerce (2004). *Obstacles to Free Trade in Canada: A Study on Internal Trade Barriers* (November).

Darby, Paul, Kip Beckman, Yves St-Maurice, and Dan Lemaire (2006). *Death by a Thousand Paper Cuts: The Effect of Barriers to Competition on Canadian Productivity.* The Conference Board of Canada.

Organisation for Economic Co-operation and Development [OECD] (2006). *Economic Survey of Canada, 2006.* Policy Brief (June). OECD.

Certified General Accountants Association of Canada (2006). *Making Trade Dispute Resolution in Canada Work: Certified General Accountants' Experience with Canada's Agreement on Internal Trade* (April). <www.cga-online.org/servlet/portal/serve/Library/News+and+Media/_Product/ca_rep_2006-05_ait.pdf>.

Dodge, David (2006). "Global Economic Forces and the Need for Adjustment." Remarks by David Dodge, Governor of the Bank of Canada, to the Chambre de commerce du Montréal métropolitain and the Fédération des chambres de commerce du Québec, Montréal, QC (June 21).

6 RED TAPE, RED INK

REDUCING REGULATION TO INCREASE PROSPERITY

A fundamental message in this volume of the Canada Strong and Free series has been that economic freedom is the most potent driver of prosperity that we know. Where economic freedom is constrained, so too are prosperity, social progress, and quality of life. As we established in chapter 2, excessive government regulation constitutes a critical constraint on economic freedom and, hence, on Canada's economic performance. If we are to achieve the best-performing economy in the world, we must address and relieve this burden.

Regulation is defined as the imposition by government of rules intended to modify economic behaviour (Jones and Graf, 2001: 7). These rules may be imposed on individuals, business and labour entities, activities, or markets. They are enforced by the threat or imposition of penalties. In addition to their goal of modifying behaviour, such regulations inevitably also create costs for those affected, costs that are ultimately borne by consumers and taxpayers.

The impact of regulation on business competitiveness cannot be emphasized enough. Regulations shape the environment in which firms operate at every turn. They affect an entrepreneur's decision to start a business, the size of the business, and how it operates. Regulations also condition the speed at which businesses are able to respond to market changes and new opportunities. In short, they decisively affect a firm's ability to innovate and compete in the constantly evolving global marketplace.

Measuring the impact of regulation on economic activity is quite different from—and harder than—determining the impacts of taxation and public spending (Jones and Graf, 2001: 3). These latter activities are highly visible, typically recorded in public accounts, and subject to intense scrutiny by political opponents, media, and citizens at large (Jones, 2002: 9). Regulation is less visible; it is generally far less subject to scrutiny and accountability. The economic impact of regulatory activity is also much more difficult to determine; the only fraction readily accessible is the impact of the administrative cost of enforcement (Jones and Graf, 2001: 3). Nonetheless, it is important to make the effort. As the following section shows, the results are illuminating.

THE COSTS OF REGULATION

Regulations impose two kinds of costs on business and society: direct and indirect (Jones and Graf, 2001: 3–4).

DIRECT COSTS

Direct regulatory costs can be broken down further into administrative and compliance costs. Administrative costs are those that government agencies incur in the course of overseeing and enforcing regulations. These costs appear in government budgets and are the only part of the regulatory footprint that is visible and easily measured (Jones and Graf, 2001: 3).

The second, and more significant, direct cost of regulation lies in compliance. These are costs that firms and individuals incur in order to abide by regulations. Unfortunately, governments are required neither to estimate nor to report these costs. Some call these kinds of costs "hidden taxation" (Jones and Graf, 2001: 3), since they act as an additional tax on doing business.

The Fraser Institute has attempted to measure both components of regulatory cost in Canada. Jones and Graf (2001: 4) estimated that Canadians spend about $103 billion a year, or about $13,700 per family of four, on regulatory compliance. This represents a burden of "hidden" taxation equivalent to 43% of what such an average family already pays in recognized taxes. In other words, due to government regulation, an average family's real tax burden is actually 43% higher than it appears to be.[1] The estimate of compliance costs by Jones and Graf (2001) was based on previous research by Weidenbaum and DeFina (1976), which found that for every dollar government spends to administer regulation, the private sector spends $17 to $20 to comply with it.

INDIRECT COSTS

Indirect costs refer to the price paid by individuals and businesses as they amend the choices they would otherwise freely make, in order to accommodate regulatory requirements. Indirect costs include profits foregone when regulations force a business to postpone getting a product to market (for example, to secure government approval for a drug). They include the cost of changing a product to respond to a regulatory mandate (as when labelling requirements are changed). Regulations impose additional unquantifiable costs when they prevent individuals from acting freely on their own preferences in choosing certain products or services (Jones and Graf, 2001: 4). These indirect costs multiply when excessive requirements for permits, licences, and regulatory approvals hinder innovation, delay development, and reduce both productivity and competitive flexibility.

Of course, the optimal level of regulation is not zero. Some regulations, such as those that directly protect persons, property, and the sanctity of contracts, provide important benefits. Distinguishing between "good" and "bad" regulation—determining which regulations yield a positive benefit-to-cost ratio and which do not—is at the heart of effective regulatory reform.

The challenge is the same we encountered earlier when considering the size of government: to strike the right balance between free economic

---

1   Figures in this section from Jones and Graf, 2001 supplemented with unpublished data from The Fraser Institute for Tax Freedom Day, 1997.

choice and regulation that truly carries a net benefit. As with the "optimal" size of government, that balance is critical to achieving for Canadians the best economic performance and quality of life.

It is beyond the scope of this study to determine the benefit/cost ratio of every category of regulation, let alone of the host of specific rules in force in Canada. What we propose instead is to examine the overall regulatory burden on Canada's citizens and their businesses in comparison with that imposed on their competitors in other OECD countries, Singapore, and Hong Kong. As proxies for this purpose, we will examine regulations that affect the start-up, operation, and termination of a business, and the property rights that are the foundations of all business.

WHERE WE STAND: INTERNATIONAL COMPARISONS

Our data for this inquiry come from two sources:

✦ The *Global Competitiveness Report*, published annually by the World Economic Forum.[2] These data are based on a survey of business decision-makers in each country.

✦ The World Bank's recently created database, *Doingbusiness: Benchmarking Business Regulations* (2005), which measures the actual requirements placed on businesses in various countries and their associated costs.

GLOBAL COMPETITIVENESS REPORT

The *Global Competitiveness Report* ranks the countries it surveys on a number of indicators, including the following three aspects of business regulation.

---

2   Note that the data from the World Economic Forum used in this section were taken from Gwartney and Lawson, 2006.

1 *Burden of Regulations:* the burden imposed by such requirements as business permits, regulations, and reporting.

2 *Time with Government Bureaucracy*: an indication by senior managers who rate, on a scale of 1 to 7, whether they have to spend a substantial amount of time dealing with government bureaucracy.

3 *Irregular Payments:* an impression of the extent to which irregular payments must be made to secure such normal business requirements as import and export permits, business licences, currency exchange, tax assessments, police protection, or loan approvals.

As can be seen from Table 6.1:

1 Twelve countries impose a lighter administrative burden on business enterprises than Canada. Canada ranks thirteenth (tied with Japan and Portugal) on this scale, out of 32 countries (30 OECD plus Hong Kong and Singapore).

2 In 14 countries, senior managers spend less time with bureaucracy than they do in Canada.

3 With respect to demands for irregular payments as conditions of regulatory approvals—an arbitrary practice that generates uncertainty and opens the door to corruption—Canada ranked seventeenth (tied with Netherlands and Portugal) in 2004. In other words, irregular payments were viewed as less frequent in 16 other countries.

DOINGBUSINESS: BENCHMARKING BUSINESS REGULATIONS

The data from *Doingbusiness: Benchmarking Business Regulations* focuses on three specific areas of regulation: the requirements to start a business, to close a business, and licences. Each of these is broken down further into components (Table 6.2, pages 72–73).

TABLE 6.1: BUSINESS REGULATIONS

	Burden of Regulations		Time with Government Bureaucracy		Irregular Payments	
	Score	Rank	Score	Rank	Score	Rank
Australia	3.0	20	5.3	21	6.3	7
Austria	3.3	16	5.9	9	6.2	10
Belgium	2.2	31	5.9	9	5.4	24
Canada	**3.4**	**13**	**5.6**	**15**	**6.0**	**17**
Czech Rep.	2.8	23	6.3	6	4.8	27
Denmark	4.0	5	5.2	22	6.4	5
Finland	4.5	3	6.8	1	6.5	3
France	2.8	23	5.4	18	5.9	20
Germany	2.7	28	5.0	25	6.1	13
Greece	2.8	23	4.9	27	4.7	29
Hong Kong, China	4.8	2	4.3	29	5.9	20
Hungary	2.9	22	6.8	1	5.4	24
Iceland	4.4	4	6.4	4	6.7	1
Ireland	3.8	6	6.0	8	6.1	13
Italy	2.1	32	5.8	13	5.5	23
Japan	3.4	13	6.4	4	6.2	10
Luxembourg	3.3	16	6.2	7	6.3	7
Mexico	2.5	30	2.8	32	4.4	30
Netherlands	3.1	19	4.5	28	6.0	17
New Zealand	3.2	18	5.5	17	6.7	1
Norway	3.5	10	5.6	16	6.4	5
Poland	2.7	28	5.2	22	4.3	31
Portugal	3.4	13	3.8	31	6.0	17
Singapore	5.4	1	5.9	9	6.5	3
Slovak Rep	2.8	23	5.4	18	4.8	27
South Korea	3.8	6	5.0	25	4.9	26
Spain	3.5	10	5.4	18	5.6	22
Sweden	3.5	10	6.5	3	6.2	10
Switzerland	3.8	6	5.9	9	6.1	13
Turkey	2.8	23	3.9	30	4.3	31
United Kingdom	3.0	20	5.8	13	6.3	7
United States	3.6	9	5.2	22	6.1	13

Note: Scores on a scale of 1 to 7; higher scores indicate less regulation. Rank out of 32.
Source: Gwartney and Lawson, 2006.

The "starting a business" area measures the general requirements to start a business in each country: the number of procedures, their cost, the time needed to complete them, and minimal capital required. Canada ranks first, implying that Canada, of all OECD countries, is the easiest place to start a business. It takes only three days to complete the two principal procedures required and costs less than 1% of average per-capita income to start a business in Canada.

The "closing a business" area measures both the cost and time required to terminate a business, and the recovery rate once a business fails. Here, Canada ranks fourth out of 31 countries (OECD plus Hong Kong and Singapore). Only Japan (first), Singapore (second), and Norway (third) do relatively better. These data show that it takes almost ten months and 4% of the value of the business to close a business in Canada. By comparison, it takes just over seven months and 4% of the estate to close a business in Japan. It takes somewhat longer to close a business in Singapore (ten months) and Norway (11 months) but costs less (1% of the estate). The OECD countries where closing a business is most difficult are the Czech Republic and Turkey, where it takes nine and six years, respectively.

Canada scores poorly, however, on "licensing requirements." Compared on the time and expense of acquiring all the licences and permits needed to build a warehouse, Canada ranks twelfth out of 31 countries (OECD plus Hong Kong and Singapore). It should be noted that the test case for Canada was Toronto, where it was determined to take 87 days on average to complete the 15 necessary procedures, at a cost of 123% of per-capita income—that is, the average income of each person in the nation. Experience may be different elsewhere in Canada.

WHEN LESS IS MORE: THE BENEFITS
OF LIGHTER REGULATION

Both the direct and indirect costs of regulation make firms less efficient and thus less competitive. Regulations that are too restrictive make it difficult to reallocate capital and labour in a timely way to respond with agility to market changes. Either way these costs are ultimately paid by

TABLE 6.2: STARTING AND CLOSING A BUSINESS AND DEALING WITH LICENCES

	Starting a Business				
	Procedures (number)	Time (days)	Cost (% of income per capita)	Min. capital (% of income per capita)	Rank (out of 31)
Australia	2	2	1.9	0.0	2
Austria	9	29	5.7	61.5	22
Belgium	4	34	11.1	13.5	16
Canada	**2**	**3**	**0.9**	**0.0**	**1**
Czech Republic	10	40	9.5	39.0	24
Denmark	3	5	0.0	47.0	11
Finland	3	14	1.2	28.0	12
France	7	8	1.2	0.0	9
Germany	9	24	4.7	47.6	20
Greece	15	38	24.6	121.4	31
Hong Kong, China	5	11	3.4	0.0	6
Hungary	6	38	22.4	79.6	23
Iceland	5	5	2.9	17.1	10
Ireland	4	24	5.3	0.0	8
Italy	9	13	15.7	10.8	18
Japan	11	31	10.7	75.3	25
Korea	12	22	15.2	308.8	29
Mexico	9	58	15.6	13.9	26
Netherlands	7	11	13.0	64.6	17
New Zealand	2	12	0.2	0.0	4
Norway	4	13	2.7	27.0	13
Poland	10	31	22.2	220.1	28
Portugal	11	54	13.4	39.4	30
Singapore	6	6	1.1	0.0	5
Slovak Republic	9	25	5.1	41.0	21
Spain	10	47	16.5	15.7	27
Sweden	3	16	0.7	35.0	14
Switzerland	6	20	8.7	31.3	15
Turkey	8	9	27.7	20.9	19
United Kingdom	6	18	0.7	0.0	7
United States	5	5	0.5	0.0	3

Note 1: Luxembourg has been excluded.

Note 2: For details on how ranks are computed, see "Ease of Doing Business: An Appendix" at

Source: World Bank, 2005.

Closing a Business				Dealing with Licences			
Time (years)	Cost (% of estate)	Recovery rate (cents on the dollar)	Rank (out of 31)	Procedures (number)	Time (days)	Cost (% of income per capita)	Rank (out of 31)
1.0	8.0	80.0	13	16	121	12.3	6
1.1	18.0	73.4	18	14	195	81.6	20
0.9	4.0	86.7	8	15	184	64.1	18
0.8	**4.0**	**90.1**	**4**	**15**	**87**	**123.0**	**12**
9.2	14.0	17.9	30	31	245	16.1	26
3.3	9.0	63.0	22	7	70	71.3	3
0.9	4.0	89.1	5	17	56	76.2	10
1.9	9.0	47.7	24	10	185	78.3	13
1.2	8.0	53.0	23	11	165	82.8	11
2.0	9.0	46.0	26	17	176	71.9	21
1.1	9.0	81.2	12	22	230	38.5	25
2.0	14.0	35.8	29	25	213	279.1	29
1.0	4.0	81.7	10	20	124	16.8	16
0.4	9.0	88.0	6	10	181	23.6	8
1.2	22.0	40.0	27	17	284	147.3	27
0.6	4.0	92.7	1	11	87	19.7	2
1.5	4.0	81.7	11	14	60	232.6	14
1.8	18.0	64.1	20	12	222	159.0	22
1.7	1.0	86.7	7	18	184	142.7	24
2.0	4.0	71.0	19	7	65	29.3	1
0.9	1.0	91.1	3	13	97	53.9	5
1.4	22.0	64.0	21	25	322	83.1	30
2.0	9.0	74.7	17	20	327	57.7	28
0.8	1.0	91.4	2	11	129	24.0	4
4.8	18.0	38.6	28	13	272	18.0	19
1.0	14.0	77.9	14	12	277	77.1	23
2.0	9.0	74.9	16	8	116	119.6	7
3.0	4.0	46.9	25	15	152	59.2	15
5.9	7.0	7.2	31	32	232	368.7	31
1.0	6.0	85.3	9	19	115	70.2	17
2.0	7.0	76.3	15	19	70	16.9	9

<http://www.doingbusiness.org/Documents/C.%20Appendix_ease%20of%20doing%20business.pdf>.

consumers, through higher prices, or by employees whose jobs are lost when their employers are forced out of business.

On the other hand, empirical research demonstrates that reducing business regulation leads to more business investment and higher productivity overall. Nicoletti and Scarpetta (2003), for example, looked at the effect of regulation on both manufacturing and service industries in 18 OECD countries over the last two decades. They found that lowering barriers to entry—such as restrictive licensing, limits on foreign firms, administrative burdens, and tariff and non-tariff barriers—resulted in productivity gains. Indeed, they found that if some European countries reduced their elevated barriers to entry in service industries to the OECD average over a ten-year period, they could expect to see total factor productivity in that service sector increase by 0.1 to 0.2 percentage points.

Alesina et al. (2005) studied barriers to entry in seven utility, transportation, and telecommunications industries in 21 OECD countries from 1975 to 1998. They found that reductions in barriers to entry lead to higher levels of investment in the long run.

Bassanini and Ernst (2002) investigated the impact of regulation and non-tariff trade barriers on innovation in 18 manufacturing industries, using data from 18 OECD countries. They found that non-tariff barriers and inward-oriented regulation both had an unambiguous negative relationship with research and development. On the other hand, "stronger protection of intellectual property rights [was] positively associated with higher R&D intensity" (2002: 6).

At the extreme, the cost of complying with excessive regulation may reach a point at which a firm is better off bribing officials in order to avoid their obligations or operating in a black market. Djankov et al. (2002) found exactly this when they examined the regulation of start-up firms in 85 countries in 1999. After looking at the number of procedures and forms, time, and cost required to operate legally, they found that countries with heavier regulatory burdens also had higher levels of corruption and larger unofficial economies.[3]

---

3   They also found that a higher level of regulation of entry is not associated with higher-quality products, lower levels of pollution, or better health outcomes.

Based on these studies and Canada's rank relative to its OECD competitors according to World Economic Forum and the World Bank, we must conclude the following.

✤ In comparison with its industrialized peers, there are only two areas of business regulation in which Canada is a top performer: the requirements for starting and closing a business.

✤ If Canada places thirteenth on burden of regulation, fifteenth in the amount of time consumed with bureaucrats, and seventeenth on demands for irregular payments, there is obviously both scope and an urgent need for significant reform in each of these areas.

✤ Reducing regulation is essential to putting Canadian business enterprises in a better position to compete with those in other industrialized countries.

RECOMMENDATIONS

Canada needs to clear away the regulatory jungle that currently hampers our ability to innovate, adapt, seek out new markets for our products, and attain the achievable goal of leading the world in prosperity and quality of life. We therefore urge a fundamental change in how Canada introduces, manages, and retires business regulation and recommend the following measures.

1 *Follow up on the Smart Regulation Initiative*
In March 2005, the Government of Canada launched the Smart Regulation Initiative (Canada, Privy Council Office, 2006). "Smart" stands for Specific, Measurable, Attainable, Realistic, and Timely. This initiative's goals are to improve the effectiveness and efficiency of regulation at all levels of government by eliminating overlaps among agencies and jurisdictions, and to update old rules to reflect new realities. A key principle was to identify "best practices" in regulation both within Canada and around the world and to encourage their general adoption. The Smart Regulation Initiative should be acted on and continued.

2 *Require government officials and interest groups proposing new regulations to submit detailed benefit/cost estimates, including estimates of compliance as well as administrative costs.*

3 *Require Parliament and legislatures, or their appropriate committees, to hold regular "delegislation/deregulation" sessions where the only item of business is to strike obsolete, unnecessary, and overly restrictive laws and regulations from the books.*

4 *Enact compulsory "sunset" provisions with every new regulation.*
All new or renewed regulations should automatically expire in five years unless specifically extended for a similar term. This will oblige government to regularly re-examine its regulatory structure and determine whether individual rules still serve a useful purpose. Every level of government, as well as any public agency charged with regulatory oversight, should adopt this requirement.

7 CONCLUSION

ECONOMIC FREEDOM BENEFITS ALL CANADIANS

Some readers may have concluded that the foregoing pages are aimed only at those who are already "haves": high income earners, business owners, those with capital wealth or property. We hope the remaining pages in this volume of the Canada Strong and Free series will persuade them otherwise. The economy, after all, belongs to all of us. Canada is strongest when all Canadians prosper. As the evidence below shows, that happens when we all enjoy the greatest degree of economic, as well as civic and political, freedom.

Balance is a core Canadian value. What balance between our public and private sectors will induce the best performance from Canada's economy, on which all of our jobs, incomes, and living standards depend? What division of effort and resources among our three levels of government will deliver the peace, order, and public services essential to our quality of life at the least cost and greatest responsiveness to our desires? What balance between "perfect" freedom and the constraints necessary to a complex society will generate the highest levels of wealth- and job-creating economic performance?

Depending on your own values and perspective, your answers to these questions may differ from ours. Your prescriptions for achieving better balances may differ from ours as well. But let us all join in a serious national conversation about these questions because all will agree, we hope, that the potential payoffs for getting the answers "right" are so enormous that we should make the effort to determine and implement whatever policies will realize them.

We have argued here that finding the "optimal" balance between Canada's public and private sectors will not only generate more "bang" for our tax dollars, in terms of improved services at lower cost, but also greater economic growth with more and better employment. Removing the barriers that continue to impede our trade with other Canadians, strengthening the rule of law and property rights, reducing needless regulation and time spent fighting bureaucratic red tape are measures that will increase our ability to prosper in an increasingly competitive global economy.

But we agree that these gains will be of little value to the great majority of Canadians if they accrue to only a few. For this reason, we conclude this volume with a special emphasis on the powerful evidence that greater economic freedom leads to substantive improvement in the well-being of every citizen in a variety of ways.

THE BENEFITS OF ECONOMIC FREEDOM

Research on economic freedom may be modern but its practice is as ancient as human history and as common as the village market. The mechanics of economic freedom are easy to understand. It should be equally easy to understand why we should all aspire to the highest level of economic freedom for Canadians.

Any transaction freely entered into must benefit both parties. Any transaction that does not would surely be rejected by the party whom it disadvantages. This simple truth has consequences throughout the economy. Consumers who are free to choose will be strongly attracted by superior quality and price. A producer in a competitive market must constantly improve on both counts or innovate new products. A producer who does not will simply send business to competitors who do. Billions of mutually beneficial transactions occur every day on this basis, powering the dynamic that spurs increased productivity, creativity, and wealth around the world.

Conversely, any restraint—from confiscatory taxation to coercive limits on choice—that prevents people from freely making mutually beneficial transactions, stunts all three of those desirable outcomes.

Not surprisingly, numerous fact-based articles in top-rated peer-reviewed journals have confirmed that economic freedom promotes economic growth and prosperity, whether the study examined jurisdictions around the world or states and provinces in North America (e.g., Easton and Walker, 1997; Karabegović and McMahon, 2005).

It is important to recognize, however, that the rewards of economic freedom are not solely material. Economic freedom cannot be separated from the exercise of other liberties. When a government may determine the capacity of individual citizens to feed, clothe, house, or educate their families and themselves, whether they hold a job or start a business, with whom they may enter into a transaction or sign a contract, that government has all the power it needs to suppress other freedoms as well. When economic freedom is absent or deficient, people must depend on the favour of the state for security and advancement, even for subsistence. Economic freedom conveys independence of livelihood, empowering citizens to insist on other freedoms.

This organic connection between economic freedom, democracy, and the exercise of other freedoms has also been confirmed by empirical research (Griswold, 2004; Dawson, 1998). The following charts and commentary—based on the Economic Freedom Index published in *Economic Freedom of the World: 2006 Annual Report* (Gwartney and Lawson, 2006)—document the powerful contribution that economic freedom makes to prosperity, the reduction of poverty and inequality, and the exercise of other freedoms.

These rewards are of such enormous value to Canadians and others around the world that we should do everything in our power to identify and act upon the public policy choices that unlock them.

ECONOMIC FREEDOM PROMOTES PROSPERITY AND ECONOMIC GROWTH

In Figure 7.1, the 130 nations included in *Economic Freedom of the World: 2006 Annual Report* have been sorted into four groups (quartiles), based on their levels of economic freedom. As can be seen, nations with the most economic freedom have by far the highest GDP per capita as well as the highest GDP growth rates. Those with the least economic freedom suffer the least prosperity and lowest economic growth.

But does economic freedom really promote economic growth? Or were some nations already rich for historical reasons and economic freedom followed prosperity rather than the other way around? Is it possible that central economic planning—with its state-imposed restrictions on economic freedom—is more conducive to growth than economic freedom?

FIGURE 7.1: ECONOMIC FREEDOM AND PROSPERITY

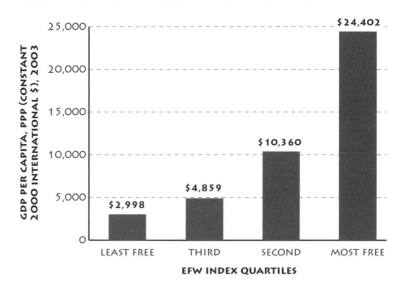

Note: Figures are in constant 2000 dollars adjusted for purchasing power parity.
Source: *Economic Freedom of the World: 2006 Annual Report.*

Figure 7.2 tells the story. It is especially striking that the least free nations (in the fourth quartile), whether their economies are centrally directed or not, are regressing—becoming poorer. At the same time, today's freest nations, regardless of their economic inheritance, continue to enjoy strong economic growth. Some jurisdictions experiencing high levels of prosperity today, for example South Korea and Ireland, were very poor until they adopted policies that significantly increased the economic freedom of their people.

ECONOMIC FREEDOM REDUCES POVERTY

Those opposed to freer markets and freedom of enterprise often argue that these create wealth for the few and poverty and repression for most. To test this thesis, we first examined the United Nations Human Poverty Index (HPI) for developing nations. This index establishes a poverty ranking for each nation based on: 1. probability at birth of not surviving to age 40;

FIGURE 7.2: ECONOMIC FREEDOM AND ECONOMIC GROWTH

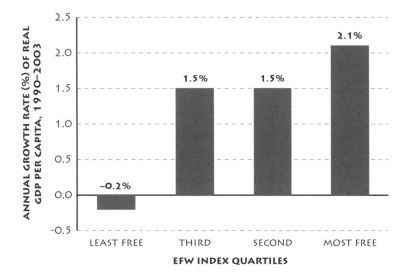

Source: *Economic Freedom of the World: 2006 Annual Report.*

2. adult literacy; 3. portion of the population without access to improved water; and 4. percentage of children underweight for their age. It is important to bear in mind that, in this formula, a low score represents less poverty; that is, more prosperity.

We then compared these poverty scores with the same nations' rankings on the Economic Freedom Index. What do we find? Those nations that have the least economic freedom also score the worst on the Human Poverty Index (see Figure 7.3).

ECONOMIC FREEDOM AND UNEMPLOYMENT

Another indicator of poverty is the ability (or inability) to find work. Figure 7.4 compares the degree of economic freedom in the world's nations to the extent of unemployment. The link is clear: the more economic

FIGURE 7.3: ECONOMIC FREEDOM AND POVERTY AS MEASURED BY THE UNITED NATIONS HUMAN POVERTY INDEX

Source: *Economic Freedom of the World: 2006 Annual Report.*

freedom, the fewer jobless. This is because, where citizens enjoy economic freedom, governments do not stand in the way of agreements, including work contracts, that are freely entered into and economic freedom unleashes job-creation energy and ingenuity.

ECONOMIC FREEDOM AND INEQUALITY

Even if a rising tide lifts all boats, it may be argued that it lifts the richest more than the poorest, increasing inequality. But, in fact, the share of national income received by the poorest appears to be largely unaffected by economic freedom and open markets and, indeed, is slightly higher in the "most free" nations than in the "least free" (Sala-i-Martin, 2002). However, the much greater prosperity in nations with more economic freedom means that the same share of the economic pie in those countries produces much greater real incomes for the poor (Figure 7.5).

FIGURE 7.4: ECONOMIC FREEDOM AND UNEMPLOYMENT

Source: *Economic Freedom of the World: 2006 Annual Report.*

FIGURE 7.5: ECONOMIC FREEDOM AND INEQUALITY

Source: *Economic Freedom of the World: 2006 Annual Report.*

ECONOMIC FREEDOM INCREASES OTHER FREEDOMS

Other empirical evidence confirms the connection between economic free-dom and other rights and liberties important to our democratic values. To demonstrate, we compared nations' economic freedom by quartile, this time with two indexes developed by Freedom House, an independent non-governmental organization that has studied and supported democratic freedoms for more than half a century (Figure 7.6). The first Freedom House Index ranks political rights, the second, civil liberties. Both indexes use a scale of 1 to 7 and higher scores mean fewer rights and liberties.

Again, greater economic freedom is undeniably associated with higher ratings on both political rights and civil liberties. Indeed, no nation that lacks economic freedom has ever supported stable political and civil freedoms. It can also be argued that no jurisdiction that has ever adopted economic freedom has failed to evolve toward political freedom, with the exceptions of Singapore and Hong Kong; and the jury is still out on them.

FIGURE 7.6: ECONOMIC FREEDOM AND OTHER FREEDOMS

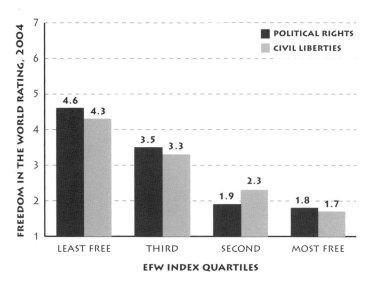

Note: Political rights and civil liberties are measured on a scale from one to seven: one = the highest degree of political rights/civil liberties; seven = the lowest.

Source: *Economic Freedom of the World: 2006 Annual Report.*

When a government has the power to determine individuals' ability to feed, clothe, house, and educate their families or to hold a job and get a promotion, and power to restrict their ability to move ahead in other ways, it has all the tools it needs to suppress democracy and other freedoms, at least until life becomes unbearable and recourse is had to violence.

Economic freedom liberates individuals from dependence on government by producing other power centres such as independent individuals, businesses, and unions. Empirical studies support the connection between economic freedom, other freedoms, and democracy.

A further comparison in many ways sums up the benefits of economic freedom. The United Nations every year releases its Human Development Index (HDI) as a global measure of a range of indicators of freedom, economic well-being, and social progress. How does that ranking compare with the index of economic freedom? Figure 7.7 tells the tale.

FIGURE 7.7: ECONOMIC FREEDOM AND THE UNITED NATIONS HUMAN DEVELOPMENT INDEX

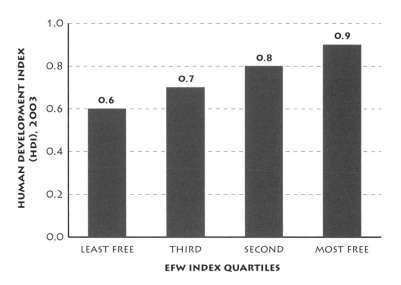

Note: The United Nations' Human Development Index (HDI) is measured on a scale from zero to one: zero = least developed; one = most developed.

Source: *Economic Freedom of the World: 2006 Annual Report.*

CONCLUSION

Can more be said and done to give Canada the best economic performance in the world as a foundation for achieving the highest quality of life in the world? Of course! We recognize that "improving economic performance" must mean more than simply increasing Canada's per-capita production of goods and services. If environmental conservation is a fundamental dimension of quality of life—as we believe it is—then economic performance must be improved in environmentally compatible ways, not at the expense of the environment for future generations. How to accomplish this—the marrying of a genuine commitment to environmental conservation with free-market approaches to economic development—is a huge challenge, but one that must be met in the days ahead. A key part of the effort will be the harnessing of market mechanisms themselves to meet demands for environmental conservation.

We further recognize the critical importance of freeing labour markets in order to optimize Canada's economic performance. This is especially necessary to meet the challenges of acute labour shortages in key sectors of our economy and to replace jobs in the old manufacturing economy with new jobs in the knowledge economy of the future. How to accomplish this is another huge challenge but, again, one that must be met in the days ahead.[1]

While this volume has focused on supporting and strengthening freedom of economic activity, we also recognize the importance of supporting freedom of scientific inquiry and the application of its results to the improvement of our economy and social services. How to accomplish this—the development of a 21st-century public-policy framework and market incentives for the support and application of science, technology, and innovation—is again a huge challenge to be met in the days ahead.

We also recognize (as pointed out in volume 1 of this series) that economic freedom is one side of a two-sided coin. The other side of the coin is the acceptance of the responsibilities and obligations that attend the exercise of that freedom. How to ensure this—the balancing of an expansion of freedom of enterprise, trade, labour, and scientific inquiry with the exercise of responsibility—is another huge challenge to be met in the days ahead.

In this volume, however, our primary focus has been on enhancing economic freedom as the single most important thing we can do to provide to Canadians the world's highest standard of living and quality of life, and to provide a solid foundation for the pursuit of all other goals and dreams.

We especially urge our fellow Canadians to recognize that this freedom of which we speak is indivisible. Economic freedom cannot be severed from freedom of conscience and religion, freedom of speech and cultural

---

1 Considerable research has been undertaken in this area by The Fraser Institute's Centre for Labour Market Studies. Its most recent publication was *An Empirical Comparison of Labour Relations Laws in Canada and the United States* (Godin et al., 2006).

expression, a free press, unfettered scientific inquiry, freedom of association, and political liberty. Those who are indifferent to a loss of freedom in one dimension may soon discover losses in other dimensions that concern them more. And those who are indifferent to their neighbour's loss of freedom may in turn find their own freedom threatened. It has rightly been said that the fight for freedom is never won and liberty only maintained by constant vigilance.

Events daily drive home to Canadians the degree to which our own freedoms—including our economic freedom—are related to those enjoyed by, or denied to, peoples elsewhere in an increasingly interdependent world. In turn, Canada has an important role to play in defending and expanding freedom internationally. We shall have more to say on this in the next volume of the Canada Strong and Free series.

Can more be done to ensure that the rewards of economic freedom are more effectively enjoyed by all, that the expansion of economic freedom internationally through liberalized trade contributes more meaningfully to the reduction of poverty and inequality in developing nations? Yes, indeed! But this cannot be accomplished by increasing foreign "aid" as it is currently conceived or by any other attempt to redistribute the output of freer economies to the less free. It can only come about through a better distribution of the means of creating wealth in the first place, by extending economic freedom itself. This means wider access to the building blocks of economic freedom: property rights, access to capital (including intellectual capital), and access to markets. More on this as well in our next volume.

Here, we conclude by returning to our starting point. Our simple goal is to make our own country, Canada, the very best place on the planet in which to live. The measures we recommend to expand our economic freedom are the most certain steps we can take toward this goal. Acted on, they will surely enrich and sustain a Canada that is truly strong and free.

REFERENCES

Afonso, Antonio, Ledger Schuknecht, and Vito Tanzi (2005). "Public Sector Efficiency: An International Comparison." *Public Choice* 123: 321–47.

Alesina, Alberto, Silvia Ardagna, Roberto Perotti, and Fabio Schiantarelli (2002). "Fiscal Policy, Profits, and Investment." *American Economic Review* 92, 3 (June): 571–89.

Alesina, Alberto, Giuseppe Nicoletti, Silvia Ardagna, and Fabio Schiantarelli (2005). "Regulation and Investment." *Journal of the European Economic Association* 3, 4 (June): 791–825.

Auerbach, Alan J. (1983). "Taxation, Corporate Financial Policy and the Cost of Capital." *Journal of Economic Literature* 21: 905–40.

Auerbach, Alan J. (1996). "Tax Reform, Capital Allocation, Efficiency, and Growth." In Henry Aaron and William Gale, edd., *Economic Effects of Fundamental Tax Reform* (Brookings Institution Press).

Barro, Robert (1990). "Government Spending in a Simple Model of Endogenous Growth." *Journal of Political Economy* 98, 5: S103–S125.

Barro, Robert (1991). "Economic Growth in a Cross Section of Countries." *Quarterly Journal of Economics* 106, 2 (May): 407–43.

Bassanini, Andrea, and Ekkehard Ernst (2002). *Labour Market Institutions, Product Market Regulations and Innovation: Cross-Country Evidence*. Economics Department Working Paper 316. Organisation for Economic Co-operation and Development.

Baylor, Maximilian, and Louis Beausejour (2004). *Taxation and Economic Efficiency: Results from a Canadian CGE Model*. Department of Finance Working Paper. [Canada] Department of Finance.

Beaulieu, Eugene, Jim Gaisford, and Jim Higginson (2003). *Interprovincial Trade Barriers In Canada: How Far Have We Come? Where Should We Go?* The Van Horne Institute.

Beaulieu, Eugene, Kenneth J. McKenzie, Jimmy Stephane Vu, and Jean-Francois Wen (2004). *Effective Tax Rates and the Formation of Manufacturing Enterprises in Canada*. Fraser Institute Digital Publication (January). <http://www.fraserinstitute.ca/shared/readmore.asp?sNav=pb&id=638>.

Becsi, Zsolt (1996). "Do State and Local Taxes Affect Relative State Growth?" *Economic Review* 81, 2 (March/April): 18–36.

Benson, Bruce, and Ronald Johnson (1986). "The Lagged Impact of State and Local Taxes on Economic Activity and Political Behaviour." *Economic Inquiry* 24 (July): 389–401.

Berggren, Niclas (1999). "Economic Freedom and Equality: Friends or Foes?" *Public Choice* 100, 3/4 (September): 203–23.

British Columbia, Department of Finance (2005a). *Budget and Fiscal Plan 2005/06*. Government of British Columbia.

British Columbia, Department of Finance (2005b). *September Update: Budget and Fiscal Plan 2005/06*. Government of British Columbia.

British Columbia, Ministry of Economic Development (2006). *Trade, Investment and Labour Mobility Agreement between British Columbia and Alberta*. <http://www.gov.bc.ca/ecdev/down/BC-AB_TILMA_Agreement-signed.pdf>.

Cai, Jinyong, and Jagadeesh Gokhale (1997). "The Welfare Loss from a Capital Income Tax." *Federal Reserve Bank of Cleveland Economic Review* 33, 1: 2–10.

Canada, Department of Finance (2004a). *Budget 2004*. Government of Canada.

Canada, Department of Finance (2004b). *Tax Expenditures and Evaluations 2004*. <http://www.fin.gc.ca/toce/2004/taxexp04_e.html>.

Canada, Department of Finance (2005a). *Budget 2005*. Government of Canada.

Canada, Department of Finance (2005b). *The Economic and Fiscal Update*. Government of Canada.

Canada, Department of Finance (2006). *The Budget Plan 2006*. Government of Canada.

Canada, Intergovernmental Affairs, Privy Council Office (2001). *The Charlottetown Accord (1992) (Unofficial Text), Summary*. <http://www.pco-bcp.gc.ca/aia/default.asp?Language=E&page=consfile&sub=TheHistory ofConstitution&Doc=charlottetown_e.htm>.

Canada, Privy Council Office (2006). *Government Directive on Regulating*. <http://www.regulation.gc.ca/default.asp?Page=report&Language= E&doc=report_e.htm>

Canada, Royal Commission on Dominion-Provincial Relations (1940). *Report of the Royal Commission on Dominion-Provincial Relations*. "Rowell-Sirois Report." King's Printer.

Canada, Royal Commission on the Economic Union and Development Prospects for Canada [Macdonald Commission] (1985). *Report on the Economic Union and Development Prospects for Canada*. Supply and Services.

Canada Revenue Agency (2006). *Your Canada Child Tax Benefit*. T4114. <http://www.cra-arc.gc.ca/E/pub/tg/t4114/README.html>.

Canadian Chamber of Commerce (2004). *Obstacles to Free Trade in Canada: A Study on Internal Trade Barriers* (November).

Certified General Accountants Association of Canada (2006). *Making Trade Dispute Resolution in Canada Work: Certified General Accountants' Experience with Canada's Agreement on Internal Trade* (April). <www.cga-online.org/servlet/portal/serve/Library/News+and+Media/_Product/ca_rep_2006-05_ait.pdf>.

Chao, Johnny C.P., and Herbert Grubel (1998). "Optimal Level of Spending and Taxation in Canada." In Herbert Grubel, ed., *How to Use the Fiscal Surplus: What is the Optimal Size of Government?* (The Fraser Institute): 53–68.

Chirinko, Robert, Steven M. Fazzari, and Andrew P. Meyer (1999). "How Responsive Is Business Capital Formation to Its User Cost? An Exploration with Micro Data." *Journal of Public Economics* 74: 53–80.

Chirinko, Robert, and Andrew Meyer (1997). "The User Cost of Capital and Investment Spending: Implications for Canadian Firms." In Paul J. N. Halpern, ed., *Financing Growth in Canada* (University of Calgary Press): 17–69.

Clemens, Jason, Joel Emes, and Rodger Scott (2002). *The Corporate Capital Tax: Canada's Most Damaging Tax*. Public Policy Sources 56 (April). The Fraser Institute.

Clemens, Jason, and Niels Veldhuis (2005). *Growing Small Businesses in Canada: Removing the Tax Barrier.* Studies in Entrepreneurship & Markets 1 (December). The Fraser Institute.

[Committee on Internal Trade] (1995). *Agreement on Internal Trade.*
<http://www.ait-aci.ca/index_en/ait.htm>.

COMPAS (2004). *Inter-Provincial Trade Barriers: Seriously Damaging to the Economy and Standard of Living and Almost as Harmful as Canada-U.S. Trade Barriers.* BDO Dunwoody/Chamber Weekly CEO/Business Leader Poll in the *Financial Post,* for Publication September 13, 2004. COMPAS Inc.

Cummins, Jason, Kevin Hassett, and Glen Hubbard (1996). "Tax Reforms and Investment: A Cross-country Comparison." *Journal of Public Economics* 62, 1-2: 237–73.

Darby, Paul, Kip Beckman, Yves St-Maurice, and Dan Lemaire (2006). *Death by a Thousand Paper Cuts: The Effect of Barriers to Competition on Canadian Productivity.* The Conference Board of Canada.

Dawson, John W. (1998). "Institutions, Investment, and Growth: New Cross-Country and Panel Data Evidence." *Economic Inquiry* 36 (October): 603–19.

Djankov, Simeon, Rafael La Porta, Florencio Lepez-de-Silanes, and Andrei Shleifer (2002). "The Regulation of Entry." *Quarterly Journal of Economics* 117, 1 (February): 1–37.

Dodge, David (2006). "Global Economic Forces and the Need for Adjustment." Remarks by David Dodge, Governor of the Bank of Canada, to the Chambre de commerce du Montréal métropolitain and the Fédération des chambres de commerce du Québec, Montréal, QC (June 21).

Doucouliagos, Chris, and Mehmet Ali Ulubasoglu (2006). "Economic Freedom and Economic Growth: Does Specification Make a Difference?" *European Journal of Political Economy* 22, 1: 60–81.

Easton, Steven T., and Michael A. Walker (1997). "Income, Growth, and Economic Freedom." *American Economic Review* 87, 2 (May): 328–32.

Emes, Joel, and Jason Clemens (2001). *Flat Tax: Principles and Issues.* Critical Issues Bulletins (April). The Fraser Institute.

Emes, Joel, and Dexter Samida (1997). "Canada's Tax on Economic Growth." Unpublished manuscript, The Fraser Institute.

Farr, W. Ken, Richard A. Lord, and J. Larry Wolfenbarger (1998). "Economic Freedom, Political Freedom and Economic Well-Being: A Causality Analysis." *Cato Journal* 18, 2 (Fall): 247–62.

Fazzari, Steven, R. Glenn Hubbard, and Bruce Petersen (1988). "Investment, Financing Decisions, and Tax Policy." *American Economic Review* 78, 2: 200–05.

Feldstein, Martin (1999). "Tax Avoidance and the Deadweight Loss of the Income Tax." *Review of Economics and Statistics* 81, 4: 674–80.

Folster, Stefan, and Magnus Henrekson (2001). "Growth Effects of Government Expenditure and Taxation in Rich Countries." *European Economic Review* 45: 1501–20.

Gartzke, Eric (2005). "Economic Freedom and Peace." In James Gwartney and Robert Lawson, *Economic Freedom of the World: 2005 Annual Report* (The Fraser Institute): 29–44.

Godin, Keith, Milagros Palacios, Jason Clemens, Niels Veldhuis, and Amela Karabegović (2006). *An Empirical Comparison of Labour Relations Laws in Canada and the United States.* Studies in Labour Markets 2. The Fraser Institute.

Goolsbee, Austan (1998). "Investment Tax Incentives, Prices, and the Supply of Capital Goods." *Quarterly Journal of Economics* 93, 1: 121–48.

Goolsbee, Austan (2004a). "Taxes and the Quality of Capital." *Journal of Public Economics* 88: 519–43.

Goolsbee, Austan (2004b). "The Impact of the Corporate Income Tax: Evidence from State Organizational Form Data." *Journal of Public Economics* 88: 2283–99.

Grady, Patrick, and Kathleen Macmillan (1998). "Why Is Interprovincial Trade Down and International Trade Up?" *Canadian Business Economics* (November): 26–35.

Gravelle, Jane (1989). "Differential Taxation of Capital Income: Another Look at the 1986 Tax Reform Act." *National Tax Journal* 42, 4: 441–63.

Gravelle, Jane (2004). "The Corporate Tax: Where Has It Been and Where Is It Going?" *National Tax Journal* 57, 4: 903–23.

Gravelle, Jane, and Laurence Kotlikoff (1993). "Corporate Tax Incidence and Inefficiency when Corporate and Noncorporate Goods Are Close Substitutes." *Economic Inquiry* 31, 4: 501–16.

Grier, Kevin, and Gordon Tullock (1989). "An Empirical Analysis of Cross-national Economic Growth, 1951–80." *Journal of Monetary Economics* 24: 259–76.

Griswold, Daniel T. (2004). *Trading Tyranny for Freedom: How Open Markets Till the Soil for Democracy.* Trade Policy Analysis 26 (January). Cato Institute.

Grossman, Philip (1988). "Government and Economic Growth: A Non-Linear Relationship." *Public Choice* 56: 193–200.

Grubel, Herbert G. (1998). "Economic Freedom and Human Welfare: Some Empirical Findings." *Cato Journal* 18, 2 (Fall): 287–304.

Grubel, Herbert G. (2000). *Unlocking Canadian Capital: The Case for Capital Gains Tax Reform.* The Fraser Institute.

Grubel, Herbert G., ed. (2001). *International Evidence on the Effects of Having No Capital Gains Taxes*. Vancouver, BC: The Fraser Institute.

Grubel, Herbert G., ed. (2003). *Tax Reform in Canada: Our Path to Greater Prosperity*. Vancouver, BC: The Fraser Institute.

Gwartney, James, Randall Holcombe, and Robert Lawson (1998). "The Scope of Government and the Wealth of Nations." *Cato Journal* 18, 2 (Fall): 163–90.

Gwartney, James, and Robert Lawson (2006). *Economic Freedom of the World: 2006 Annual Report*. The Fraser Institute. <http://www.freetheworld.com>.

Gwartney, James, Robert Lawson, and Walter Block (1996). *Economic Freedom of the World: 1975–1995*. The Fraser Institute. <http://www.freetheworld.com>.

Hall, Robert E., and Alvin Rabushka (1995). *The Flat Tax*. Hoover Institution Press.

Harris, Mike, and Preston Manning (2005). *A Canada Strong and Free*. The Fraser Institute and Montreal Economic Institute.

Hart, Michael (2004). "Lessons from Canada's History as a Trading Nation." *Fraser Forum* (June): 6–8.

Helliwell, John F. (2002). *Globalization and Well-Being*. UBC Press.

Helliwell, John F., and John McCallum (1995). "National Borders Still Matter for Trade." *Policy Options* 16: 44–48.

Helms, L. Jay (1985). "The Effect of State and Local Taxes on Economic Growth: A Time Series-Cross Section Approach." *Review of Economics and Statistics* 67, 4: 574–82.

Hendricks, Kenneth, Raphael Amit, and Diana Whistler (1997). *Business Taxation of Small and Medium-sized Enterprises in Canada.* Working Paper 97-11. Prepared for the Technical Committee on Business Taxation. [Canada] Department of Finance.

Holtz-Eakin, Douglas, and Donald Marples (2001a). *Distortion Costs of Taxing Wealth Accumulation: Income versus Estate Taxes.* Working paper 8261. National Bureau of Economic Research (NBER).

Holtz-Eakin, Douglas and Donald Marples (2001b). *Estate Taxes, Labour Supply, and Economic Efficiency.* Center for Policy Research Special Report. American Council for Capital Formation.

International Monetary Fund (2005). *World Economic Outlook: Building Institutions* (September). <http://www.imf.org/external/pubs/ft/weo/2005/02/index.htm>

Jones, Laura (2002). "Measuring the Regulatory Burden: The First Step Towards Accountability." *Fraser Forum* (January): 9, 15.

Jones, Laura, and Stephen Graf (2001). *Canada's Regulatory Burden. How Many Regulations? At What Cost?* Fraser Forum Special Issue (August).

Jorgensen, Dale W., and Kun-Young Yun (1991). "The Excess Burden of Taxation in the United States." *Journal of Accounting and Finance* 6: 487–508.

Karabegović, Amela, and Jason Clemens (2005). "Ending Child Labour—Bans Aren't the Solution." *Fraser Forum* (March): 25–26.

Karabegović, Amela, and Fred McMahon (2005). *Economic Freedom of North America: 2005 Annual Report.* The Fraser Institute.

Kesselman, Jonathan, and Finn Poschmann (2001). *A New Option for Retirement Savings: Tax-Prepaid Savings Plans.* CD Howe Institute.

King, R.G., and S. Rebelo (1990). "Public Policy and Economic Growth: Developing Neoclassical Implications." *Journal of Political Economy* 98, 5: 126–50.

Knox, Robert (1998). "Economic Integration in Canada through the Agreement on Internal Trade" In Harvey Lazar, ed., *Canada: The State of the Federation 1997; Non-constitutional Renewal* (Institute of Intergovernmental Relations, Queen's University, Kingston; McGill-Queen's University Press): 137–67.

Liu, Liqun, and Andrew Rettenmaier (2004). "The Excess Burden of the Social Security Tax." *Public Finance Review* 32, 6: 631–50.

Mackness, William (1999). *Canadian Public Spending: The Case for Smaller More Efficient Government*. Public Policy Source 13. The Fraser Institute.

Mbaku, John Mukum, ed. (1999). *Preparing Africa for the Twenty-First Century: Strategies for Peaceful Co-existence and Sustainable Development*. Ashgage.

McCallum, John. 1995. "National Borders Matter: Canada-US Regional Trade Patterns." *American Economic Review* 3: 615–23.

Mintz, Jack M., Duanjie Chen, Yvan Guillemette, and Finn Poschmann (2005). *The 2005 Tax Competitiveness Report: Unleashing the Canadian Tiger*. The CD Howe Institute.

Nicoletti, Giuseppe, and Stefano Scarpetta (2003). "Regulation, Productivity and Growth: OECD Evidence." *Economic Policy* 18, 36 (April): 9–72.

Organisation for Economic Co-operation and Development [OECD] (1997). *OECD Economic Survey: Canada*. OECD.

Organisation for Economic Co-operation and Development [OECD] (2005). *Revenue Statistics 1965–2004*. OECD.

Organisation for Economic Co-operation and Development [OECD] (2006). *OECD Economic Outlook* 79 (May). OECD.

Parsons, Graham (1994). *Internal Trade and Economic Cooperation: Down to the Wire on an Internal Trade Agreement.* Canada West Foundation.

Peden, Edgar (1991). "Productivity in the United States and Its Relationship to Government Activity: An Analysis of 57 Years, 1929–1986." *Public Choice* 69: 153–73.

Peden, Edgar, and Michael Bradley (1989). "Government Size, Productivity, and Economic Growth: The Post-War Experience." *Public Choice* 61: 229–45.

Porter, E. Michael, Klaus Schwab, Xavier Sala-i-Martin, and Augusto Lopez-Claros (2004). *Global Competitiveness Report 2004–2005.* World Economic Forum. <http://www.palgrave.com/products/Catalogue.aspx?is=1403949131>.

Razin, Assaf, and Chin-Wa Yuen (1996). "Capital Income Taxation and Long-Run Growth: New Perspectives." *Journal of Public Economics* 59: 239–63.

Sala-i-Martin, Xavier. 2002. The Disturbing "Rise" of Global Income Inequality. NBER Working Paper No. 8904 (April). <http://papers.nber.org/papers/w8904>.

Schuknecht, Ludger, and Vito Tanzi (2005). *Reforming Public Expenditure in Industrialised Countries: Are There Trade-Offs?* Working paper 435 (February). European Central Bank.

Scully, Gerald W. (1989). "The Size of the State, Economic Growth and the Efficient Utilization of National Resources." *Public Choice* 63: 149–64.

Scully, Gerald W. (1991). *Tax Rates, Tax Revenues and Economic Growth.* Policy Report 98. National Center for Policy Analysis.

Scully, Gerald W. (1994). *What Is the Optimal Size of Government in the United States?* Policy Report 188. National Center for Policy Analysis.

Scully, Gerald W. (1995). "The 'Growth Tax' in the United States." *Public Choice* 85: 71–80.

Scully, Gerald W. (1998). *Measuring the Burden of High Taxes*. Policy Report 215. National Center for Policy Analysis.

Scully, Gerald W. (2000). *Public Spending and Social Progress*. Policy Report 232. National Center for Policy Analysis.

Social Development Canada (2006). *Social Security Statistics Canada and the Provinces, 1978-79 to 2002-03*. <http://www.sdc.gc.ca/en/cs/sp/sdc/socpol/tables/page00.shtml>. Updated by special request.

Statistics Canada (1998). *Interprovincial Trade in Canada, 1984–1996*. Statistics Canada.

Statistics Canada (2000). *Interprovincial and International Trade in Canada, 1992–1998* (June). Statistics Canada.

Statistics Canada (2002). *Provincial Trade Patterns*. Statistics Canada.

Statistics Canada (2004). *The Performance of Interprovincial and International Exports by Province and Territory since 1992* (March). Statistics Canada.

Statistics Canada (2006). Provincial Economic Accounts. Statistics Canada.

Statistics Canada, Public Institutions Division (2003). Financial Management System. Statistics Canada.

Statistics Canada, Public Institutions Division (2004). Financial Management System. Statistics Canada.

Statistics Canada, Public Institutions Division (2005). Financial
Management System. Statistics Canada.

Statistics Canada, Public Institutions Division (2006). Financial
Management System. Statistics Canada.

Tanzi, Vito (1995). *Government Role and the Efficiency of Policy Instruments*.
IMF Working Paper. International Monetary Fund.

Tanzi, Vito (2005). "The Economic Role of the State in the 21st Century."
Cato Journal 25, 3 (Fall): 617–38.

Tanzi, Vito, and Ludger Schuknecht (1997a). "Reconsidering the Fiscal
Role of Government: The International Perspective." *American Economic
Review* 87: 164–68.

Tanzi, Vito, and Ludger Schuknecht (1997b). "Reforming Government:
An Overview of the Recent Experience." *European Journal of Political
Economy* 13: 395–417.

Tanzi, Vito, and Ludger Schuknecht (1998a). "Can Small Governments
Secure Economic and Social Well-Being?" In Herbert Grubel, ed., *How to
Use the Fiscal Surplus: What is the Optimal Size of Government?* (The Fraser
Institute): 69–92.

Tanzi, Vito, and Ludger Schuknecht (1998b). "The Growth of Government
and the Reform of the State in Industrial Countries." In Andres
Solimano, ed., *Social Inequality* (Michigan University Press).

Treff, Karin, and David B. Perry (2001). *Finances of the Nation, 2000*.
Canadian Tax Foundation.

Treff, Karin, and David B. Perry (2002). *Finances of the Nation, 2001*.
Canadian Tax Foundation.

Treff, Karin, and David B. Perry (2006). *Finances of the Nation, 2005.* Canadian Tax Foundation.

US Department of Commerce, Bureau of Economic Analysis (2006). Various data series. <http://www.bea.gov/>.

US Government Accountability Office [US GAO] (2005). *Tax Policy: Summary of Estimates of the Costs of the Federal Tax System.* GAO.

Vedder, Richard K. (1993). *Economic Impact of Government Spending: A 50-State Analysis.* Policy Report 178. National Center for Policy Analysis.

Vedder, Richard K., and Lowell E. Gallaway (1998). "Government Size and Economic Growth." Paper prepared for the Joint Economic Committee of the US Congress.

Veldhuis, Niels (2006). "Presentation to The British Columbia Provincial Sales Tax Review Panel, January 19, 2006." The Fraser Institute. Available upon request.

Veldhuis, Niels, and Jason Clemens (2006). *Productivity, Prosperity, and Business Taxes.* Studies in Economic Prosperity 3. The Fraser Institute.

Walker, Michael A. (1997). "Is There an Ideal Size of Government and What Is It?" Presentation at Annual Congress of the Friedrich Naumann Stiftung.

Weidenbaum, Murray L., and Robert DeFina (1976). *The Cost of Federal Regulation of Economic Activity.* Competitive Enterprise Institute.

World Bank (2005). *Doingbusiness: Benchmarking Business Regulations* [database]. <http://www.doingbusiness.org/>.